THE JACKPOT
A Folk-Play
In Four Acts

by
Sholem Aleichem

Translated by
Kobi Weitzner
and
Barnett Zumoff

Published by the Workmen's Circle Education Department

Copyright © 1989
by Kobi Weitzner and Barnett Zumoff

ALL RIGHTS RESERVED

CAUTION: Professionals and amateurs are hereby warned that THE JACKPOT is subject to a royalty. It is fully protected under the copyright laws of the United States of America, the British Commonwealth, including Canada, and all other countries of the Copyright Union. All rights, including professional, amateur, motion pictures, recitation, lecturing, public reading, radio broadcasting, television, are strictly reserved. In its present form the play is dedicated to the reading public only.

THE JACKPOT may be given stage presentation by amateurs upon payment of a royalty of Sixty Dollars for the first peformance, and Forty Dollars given, to Kobi Weitzner, 161 West 106th Street, Apt. 3W, New York, N.Y. 10025, Phone: (212) 864-1789 or to Barnett Zumoff, 3710 Bedford Avenue, Brooklyn, N.Y. 11229, Phone: (718) 252-7976.

Royalty of the required amount must be paid whether the play is presented for charity or gain and whether or not admission is charged.

Stock royalty quoted on application to Kobi Weitzner and Barnett Zumoff.

For all other rights than those stipulated above, apply to Kobi Weitzner and Barnett Zumoff.

Particular emphasis is laid on the question of amateur or professional readings, permission and terms for which must be secured in writing from Kobi Weitzner and Barnett Zumoff.

Copying from this book in whole or in part is strictly forbidden by law, and the right of performance is not transferable.

Whenever the play is produced the following notice must appear on all programs, printing and advertising for the play: "Produced by special arrangement with Kobi Weitzner and Barnett Zumoff."

The publication of this play does not imply that it is necessarily available for performance by amateurs or professionals. Amateurs and professionals considering a production are strongly advised in their own interests to apply to Kobi Weitzner and Barnett Zumoff before starting rehearsals, advertising, or booking a theatre or hall.

No part of this book may be reproduced, stored in a retrieval system, or transmitted in any form, by any means, including mechanical, electronic, photocopying, recording, or otherwise, without the prior permission of the publisher.

Printed in U.S.A.

Table of Contents

Introduction 7
First Act 19
Second Act 39
Third Act 67
Fourth Act 91
Text Sources 105
Bibliography in Yiddish and Hebrew 105
Bibliography in Other Languages 106
Bibliography 106

We would like to thank Professor Mikhl Herzog, Professor Chone Shmeruk, Moishe Rosenfeld, Renee Raskin and Dr. Chava Lapin for their invaluable advice and assistance in the preparation of this translation.

THE JACKPOT

*A Folk-Play
In Four Acts*

INTRODUCTION

Sholem Aleichem is to Yiddish literature what Mark Twain is to American literature — the great master. Known in world literature as a story teller, his dramatic work passed almost unnoticed. This is the first English translation of a Sholem Aleichem play.

The Jackpot was written by Sholem Aleichem in 1914, two years before his death. It is Sholem Aleichem's best comedy. Contrary to the common myth that Sholem Aleichem wrote effortlessly, *The Jackpot* was not written in one draft. The manuscript kept in the Sholem Aleichem Archive in Tel Aviv is covered with several layers of changes written on paper strips and neatly cut and glued. Sholem Aleichem did not leave, and probably did not write, more than one version of the play. Still, for a while he considered a different behavior for Beylke, the ingenue in the play. In two alternative versions to acts three and four, Sholem Aleichem made Beylke absolutely passive. This, however, was not in keeping with her character. The young women in Sholem Aleichem's dramas always have some degree of education and independent personalities. *The Jackpot* is the most urban of Sholem Aleichem's plays. *Tevye* takes place in a village and *The Gold Diggers* takes place in a little town; *The Jackpot* takes place in a city. In *The Gold Diggers* there is a money lender; in *The Jackpot* there are banks. Perhaps it was for that reason that, on second thought, Sholem Aleichem rejected a passive character for Beylke. It was hardly plausible that she, the city girl, would show less self-awareness than her sisters in the little town and village.

The Jackpot is Sholem Aleichem's best play also because it didn't suffer from the interference of the theater managers of New York, like *Stempenyu*. Sholem Aleichem was forced to give a melodramatic polish to the heroine in *Stempenyu*. "A Jewish woman doesn't poison herself over a love affair," he wrote in a letter to his son-in-law, "but what can I do when America gives an order?"

Seven years later, by the time Sholem Aleichem came out with *The Jackpot,* the Yiddish theater managers in New York, disappointed by the financial failures of his previous plays, were no longer interested in his work. Consequently Sholem Aleichem was under no pressure from them to make the play more "commercial." This probably helped to preserve the quality of the play.

Sholem Aleichem died before his play was performed. After his death, *The Jackpot* became a classic piece in the small repertory of the Yiddish theater. It was the central production in the Moscow Yiddish Chamber Theater, the only Yiddish state theater in the period between the two World Wars, and it became a favorite in what survived of the Yiddish theater after the Second World War.

THE JACKPOT in the Moscow State Theater with the Director Alexander Granovsky

Alexander Granovsky was the great innovator of the European Yiddish theater. A disciple of the Jewish-Austrian director Max Reinhardt, he brought the Yiddish theater from vaudeville to the big leagues of international theater.

Granovsky changed the face of the Russian Yiddish theater, which until that time had presented mainly "shund" plays. Shund plays are a potpourri of sensational plots interspersed with low comedy, melodrama, songs and dances, erotic innuendos, and religious kitsch — supposedly a recipe for commercial success. In that type of theater, the text is of no consequence, and the only thing that counts is the star. In shund performances, to this day,

INTRODUCTION

the public applauds favorite actors whenever they appear on stage, in complete disregard of the play and the other actors on stage. The idea of stage discipline was and is alien to the Yiddish shund-theater. Every actor tried to outplay the others and steal the show. Granovsky brought to the Yiddish theater the idea of stage discipline and teamwork. The image of a loosely organized band was transformed by him into that of a symphonic orchestra. It was no longer a theater that gesticulated and improvised. Overall planning replaced pot-luck. All the theatrical ingredients — text, acting, movement — were organized into a continuity of significant images. Sholem Aleichem's drama found in him an unorthodox but inspiring interpreter.

Class Division — Space Division

Faithful to his mission as a Soviet director, Granovsky divided the characters of the play into two opposing categories, Good and Bad, as did another ideological theater, the medieval one. In the medieval theater, the spiritual division was expressed by a physical division of the stage into two levels. The upper level was Paradise and the lower level was Hell. On the upper level, God sat surrounded by white-winged angels singing Hallelujah in celestial harmony, and on the lower level Satan and his devils dwelt amid the smoke of boiling tar and the screams of the penitent sinners. Granovsky used constructivist stage design for that purpose. Conventional stage design serves as a background, and is intended to give an illusion of a location such as a forest or a street. In Granovsky's production, the stage design was a construction that the actors could sit on, jump from, and hang onto. The rich men were always down in the lower, earthly level of the stage. Their full bellies and fat buttocks pulled them downward. The have-nots, the workers, and the musicians jumped lightly on the high planks of the set. In the workshop scenes, the stage space was open and one had the sensation of freedom, whereas in the scenes that took place in the living-rooms of the rich, Granovsky enclosed the space with planks and drapes, thereby creating a feeling of suffocation. The movements of the actors blended with the stage design. The rich men moved with their limbs drooping down. The movement of the laborers flowed in symmetrical opposition, always upwards. In the scenes in tailor's shops, the workers had straight backs, and their arms were vigorously lifted up in choreographed movements as they sewed with imaginary needles and thread. In this way Granovsky created an identification of work with joy.

Beyond the Text

Granovsky did not use the actors as interpreters of the text, but as commentators who gave new meaning to it. One of Granovsky's acting devices became almost a trademark of Jewish theater and film: the flying matchmaker. Granovsky showed with symbolic body movements the parasitic position of the matchmaker in society, and his divorce from any productive activity. Soloveitchik the matchmaker was, in one word, said this time with sharp criticism, a "luftmentsh," a person who wheels and deals with nothing, with air. Thus Soloveitchik appears in Granovsky's production, hanging in the air, swinging between Heaven and Earth, jumping with his umbrella on the town's roofs.

In the work of the director Granovsky and the actor Michoels in the role of Shimele — the poor tailor who wins the jackpot — one can find concrete examples of the visual language of Granovsky. The Soviet actor and director Liubomirsky describes the text beyond the text, which shaped significant episodes in the performance. Liubomirsky describes the scene where Shimele gets the news that he has won the jackpot. Granovsky used movement as commentary on the text; the result was a powerful, grotesque image:

"The scene where Saroker gets the news of the jackpot is unforgettable. Shimele is so dazzled that his legs cave in. He is neither standing nor sitting. His daughter, Beylke, puts something on his head that looks like a sack tied at one end. Actually it is not a sack, but rather a triangular homentash (Purim pastry)...

Suddenly Saroker tears himself from his strange paralysis, straightens up, and assumes the pose of a sort of Napoleon. No more silence. He starts talking. 'You wait!' he proudly announces. 'I will show you who Shimele Saroker is, and what Shimele can do!' At first this comic metamorphosis looks wildly strange. But try to watch the Shimele character closely, and the philosophy of the 'nouveau riche' will unfold in front of you in all its glory."

Another episode where the character of Shimele Saroker gets a grotesque dimension through the movement of the actor takes place when Shimele signs the check that will rob him of the money he won.

"Whoever saw the performance will not forget the moment when Shimele signs the check. Michoels demonstrates clearly what an illiterate Shimele is — even signing the check is a hard task for him. He has to make such a huge effort that his tongue comes out of his mouth! Furthermore, in this effort he lifts his left foot off the ground. Those movements bear witness that Saroker is a big child."

Granovsky took advantage of the specificity of the theater as a point of encounter between the concrete and the abstract, between the words and the ideas on the one hand, and the live actor on the other. He disturbed the modus vivendi between the two, and made them clash. The words developed a plastic dimension. At the same time, the physical body and movement of the actor took on literal and dramatic significance.

Attacking the Tradition is an Old Jewish Tradition

Granovsky completely changed the face of the Jewish theater. However, he did not work in a vacuum. He was a revolutionary, but a revolutionary of the Jewish theater. As Sartre remarked, a Jewish French atheist is not the same as a gentile French atheist. The Jew denies the existence of the Jewish God. The French denies the existence of the Trinity. The two are different because their denial is different. Granovsky did not satirize an abstract society, he satirized Jewish society. When in whimsical spite he created the character of the Jewish matchmaker, he did not draw an abstract caricature, but a Jewish one. Soloveitchik the Matchmaker tiptoes on the stage because that is the way the Jewish idiom goes, the matchmaker *dances* at all the weddings, which means that he has a finger in every pot. He does not walk or jump, he dances. The grotesque of Granovsky was Jewish just as the fantasy of Chagal was. When the Moscow Jewish Chamber Theater appeared in Berlin, it received a particularly warm write-up from the writer Joseph Roth. In his article, Roth related to the conflict between tradition and revolution in the work of the visiting Jewish Theater:

"This is the childhood disease of the Yiddish theater, and that of the Russian revolution as a whole. The theater remains Jewish even when it attacks Jewish traditions. Attacking the tradition is an old Jewish tradition. I was moved even when they mocked. They mock, but they mock in a Jewish way. They are genuine, as genuine as the children of Israel were when Moses smashed the Ten Commandments."

Yankev Rotboym Directs

The work of the director Yankev Rotboym represents another important chapter in the theatrical history of *The Jackpot*. His sister, Leah Rotboym, was one of the principal actresses in the Moscow State Theater. The young Rotboym went to the Soviet Union to see Granovsky's work, and this included his production of *The Jackpot (200,000)*.

Rotboym became part of the brief golden age of the Yiddish theater between the two World Wars. He was called upon to direct in the "Vilner Trupe" (Vilna Troupe) when the ensemble found itself in limbo after the astounding success of *The Dybbuk*. Rotboym geared the company, towards a realistic, socially engaged repertoire. He also directed in another innovative company the "Yung Teater" (The Young Theater), and during World War II he directed in North and South America until he returned to Poland in 1946.

Although Rotboym, too, pointed out the social conflict in the play, this was not his major focus. Granovsky's gay and merciless grotesque disappears in Rotboym's interpretation. A

INTRODUCTION

folksy lyrical tone takes its place. Rotboym abandons the unequivocal class division that marks Granovsky's work. His *Jackpot* is not a play about class struggle in Jewish society, but a play about Jewish existence, with a sympathetic attitude to the working-class characters. Justifying his concept, Rotboym uses Sholem Aleichem's definition of the play: — A folk play.

The Characters

Like Granovsky before him, Rotboym gives his own interpretation to the play by giving his own interpretation to the characters. Granovsky submerged the individuals into symbols of their social classes. Rotboym returned to what was considered an abomination by the Soviets, that is to the individual psychology of the heroes. Naturally, he dealt with the psychology of the characters within the limits allowed by comedy. He did not — says Rotboym in an interview I had with him — turn the text upside down and make a psychological drama of it.

The Lyrical Theater After the War

After World War II, the critical approach to Jewish society that was typical of the progressive Yiddish theater changed completely. The attitude towards Jewish life, which was in great part exterminated during the war, became nostalgic and lyrical. The melodic music of Kahn and the poetic lyrics of Broderzon written for Rotboym's first direction of the play in 1931 with the Vilner Trupe lent themselves perfectly to the re-creation, on the stage, of the lost shtetl.

The songs helped Rotboym to keep the lyrical aspect of Shimele's character even in his new bourgeois disguise. Unlike Granovsky's Shimele, or the forefather of all Shimeles, Monsieur Jourdain in Moliere's *Le Bourgeois Gentilhomme,* Shimele in Rotboym's production does not try to erase his plebeian past. True, he wants to mingle with his new class and he adopts a Russian name, but he is still the same sympathetic person he used to be. Shimele, in the Sholem Aleichem text, is a mixture of the nouveau riche of European comedy with the Sholem Aleichem dreamer. Rotboym kept both aspects of the character. Rotboym's Shimele remains a "mentsh," a human being.

For example, when the tailor's apprentices Motl and Kopl finally succeed, after bribing the doorman, in gaining access to Shimele, Rotboym emphasizes the camaraderie that exists between the former tailor and his apprentices in spite of the class difference that now divides them.

The Rich Man Fein — Granovsky and Rotboym

In Granovsky's production, the tailor's wife, Eti Meni, looks at the world of the rich through a pince-nez made out of two bagels. In Rotboym's production, she wears feathers and a delicate golden pince-nez. The same distance that separates the Eti Meni of Granovsky's farce from the Eti Meni of Rotboym's social comedy separates the characterizations of the rich man Fein in the two versions. Here the prop that makes the difference visual is a hat. In Granovsky's production, Mr. Fein wears a huge stovepipe hat. Rotboym's Mr. Osher Fein wears a small, elegant bowler hat. There is a theatrical saying that the hat can make the role. Sometimes the actor finds the key to a character through a seemingly insignificant prop. In the comparison between Granovsky's and Rotboym's works, the difference in the props can tell us a lot about the difference in the interpretation. Rotboym brings the Feins back from the sphere of the grotesque to a rendition closer to the Sholem Aleichem text. The Feins, as indicated by their name, are the incarnation of fine taste. Rotboym follows Sholem Aleichem, and does not go beyond amused irony in his interpretation of the couple.

For Rotboym, a so-called progressive director, the bourgeoisie is still the enemy, but his is a far cry from the total war declared by Granovsky. The rich man Fein, who was, in Granovsky's production, but a brush stroke in the grotesque picture of bourgeois society, regains a human face under Rotboym's direction. In the 1973 production in Warsaw, the actor Szymon Szurmiej followed an idea of Rotboym's and gave an original presentation of the character Fein. This time the wealthy man was shown, not with a big belly and a thundering voice, but as a sickly, elegant Jew. After the placard-like theater of Granovsky, Rotboym returned the Jewish theater to nuance, to half-tone. Although a leftist himself, his style was a reaction to the black-and-white picture presented in the Soviet theater. Rotboym explains:

"With Szymon I had an interesting story. I always presented Fein as a high-class person who has a lot of money and eats very well. And all the actors were similar fat-looking Jews. I always had a hard time getting Szymon to rehearsals. He was the head of the theater. I gave him a role and he gave me a hard time. Once when he did not show up for a rehearsal, I went to his office. He said to me: 'Oy I have got a cold, oy I can't walk, it hurts here...' I said to him: 'Play Fein the way you are! Fein can be sick.' He said: 'What do you mean sick?!' I said: 'The same way you are sick now, he will be sick.' I dragged him to the stage, gave him a stick, and he came on stage this way (Rotboym demonstrates by walking bent, leaning heavily on the stick, and sitting down with a heavy sigh.) Today he plays this way. In perfect health, he plays a sick man. It is very interesting. The idea came from an incident. The rich man has a million dollars but he has a sick stomach and a weak heart."

Rotboym's sick rich man is a sick individual and at the same time the representative of a sick social class. Granovsky used the grotesque style to convey ideological messages; Rotboym shows that a realistic approach can also be ideologically charged.

"At the same time he is a symbol of a sick social class. This is not a play about class struggle. Sholem Aleichem did not write about class struggle. But it is a plebeian play; this you will find in my interpretation."

Vigdorchuk and Rubinchik

The two con men who rob Shimele of his money both come from professions that relate to the theater. One is an ex-musician, and the other a wig-maker. They have an artistic predisposition to create make-believe. They lure Shimele to invest money in their movie-theater venture. They convince him in a scene where they charm him by speaking about the magic of the movies. They escape with the money he has won in the jackpot. Fraud scenes have always been a rich potential for comedy. They are pure theater, because the actor has to play one role on top of another. They are usually very colorful theatrical scenes, such as the one in *Le Bourgeois Gentilhomme,* in which Monsieur Jourdain is fooled by the phony Sultan of Turkey. In impersonation scenes, the theater rediscovers for a moment the joyful synthesis between playing as in acting and playing as in fun and games. It is particularly surprising, therefore, that Rotboym chose to cut the fraud scene and the characters of the two charlatans who carry it out.

Yet, Rotboym was not the only director to cut that scene out. Peter Frei, who directed the play in the Hebrew "Ohel" Theater, knew the original Sholem Aleichem text and yet used the Berkovitz version, which omitted the fraud scene completely. Frei made this choice for dramatic reasons. The fraud scene is almost half an hour long, and opens a kind of play within a play — he explained. This slows down the rhythm of the performance as a whole. Frei thought that the two characters were too flat, and did not justify the focus Sholem Aleichem gave them in the original play. Frei explained:

"I found that Berkovitz's adaptation was more accomplished. He opened and closed in a smaller circle than Sholem Aleichem, but thereby accomplished a certain perfection. In Sholem Aleichem's original play, the entrance of those two good-for-nothings who sell Shimele on the idea of silent movies, of film making, suddenly starts a new play out of the blue. I find this arbitrary. Furthermore, those characters are stereotypical and flat. The character of Shimele is well founded, with deep roots, like the people who surround him: Eti Meni, the daughter, the two apprentices, all the townspeople. They are all whole characters, extraordinary characters, whereas the two con men make their entrance towards the end, for a short while, and somehow it is less convincing. Maybe I was wrong. Somehow, after comparing, I decided to stick with Berkovitz"

Rotboym, like Frei, had theatrical reasons for omitting the scene. Faithful to the concept of what he called a plebeian play,

INTRODUCTION

Rotboym added music, songs, and dance. Cutting out the scene with the scoundrels left space for all that.

"Since I wanted to make a musical comedy, it would have come out too long. I had to make place for the songs. I had to cut out unnecessary things. You can mention the business with the two con men without actively presenting it. A spectator who hasn't read the play will not feel that it is missing."

But, unlike Frei, Rotboym's approach to the scene was not purely theatrical. His motivation was basically emotional, and Rotboym is the first to admit it. In the text that served him for the production with the "Vilner Trupe" in 1931, he encircled the whole scene with large question marks, and indeed he omitted the scene completely. He reintroduced it in his production in the "Folksbiene" in New York in 1943, but subsequently omitted it from the four productions he directed thereafter. The objection Rotboym had to the two characters was moral and emotional. What characterized them was cheating and fraud. These were not characters that Rotboym was keen to present in the anti-Semitic Europe before World War II, let alone after it. The two con men were too out of line with the lyrical image Rotboym wanted to create on stage.

"They are not professionals. Absolute con men. Ugly types. What do I need them for? And Shimele looks and believes them. He likes it. The audience gets the message: 'A Jew is a swindler.' Especially after the war, here in Poland or in Germany, the audience is eighty percent non-Jewish. And Jews do not want to see ugly Jews on stage."

The Lyrical Jewish Theater After the War

The Jewish Art Theater before World War II was characterized by sharp social criticism. After the war, the criticism subsided. This change was not limited to Poland. The approach to the Jewish society that was destroyed during the war has become a loving one and the tone has become lyrical. Rotboym elaborates:

"It is a problem: how to present the Jew in a world of intensified anti-Semitism. I would have done it differently before Hitler. A lot sharper. And today I do it differently. In the

Folksbiene production of 1943, Soloveitchik — the Matchmaker — looks like a clown. After the war he was fashionable, nicely dressed. I try, while directing Jewish plays, to present the Jew in a delicate way, not idealizing him or presenting him as an angel, but I would never direct Asch's *God of Vengeance* today. I would not do it for all the money in the world." (In *God of Vengeance*, a Jewish brothel-keeper who has become rich finds a respectable match for his daughter, but she chooses to become a whore instead.)

A Caged Bird

Yankev Rotboym is both a director and a landmark of theatrical history. In his work in the theater are reflected the successive eras of the Yiddish theater from the thirties to the eighties.

His work on *The Jackpot* went from the daring grotesque, a la Granovsky, to a lyrical, restrained versions after the war. The Yiddish theater in Europe, like a film that comes to its end, tries to survive by running backwards. This reverse chronology is reflected in Rotboym's work. His *Jackpot* of the Forties is far more daring and innovative than his works in the eighties. Itzik Manger wrote a poem about a mother who wraps her beloved child to protect him against the winter cold. The many layers of clothes are too heavy. The child, who wanted to be a bird, cannot fly, because of his mother's love.

The Yiddish theater after the Second World War is carefully protected by the surviving directors. The idea is to take loving care of what is left. Aggression, spite, carefree humor, and biting satire, in other words the stuff good theater is made of, are banned. Rotboym is part of this trend and his case is particularly striking. His later productions are a reaction to his own, early work.

Kobi Weitzner

THE CAST

Shimele Saroker: A tailor, son of a tailor, middle-aged, with a lovely voice.

Eti Meni: His wife, a peculiar woman.

Beylke: Their daughter, a beauty.

Motl Kasoy:
Kopl Falbon: Tailor's apprentices. Guys with guts.

Oscar Solomonovich (Osher) Fein: A rich Jew, an aristocrat, bald with a pot-belly.

Gertruda Grigorevna (Golde) Fein: His wife — pale and sickly-looking.

Solomon Oskarovich Fein: Their son, a handsome young man.

Koltun: A bill-collector for the Feins' tenement houses. Single and unattractive.

Soloveitchik: A worldly matchmaker. Wears a bowler.

Goldenthaler: A director of a bank.

Himmelfarb: A bookkeeper with a gift of gab.

Vigdorchuk: An ex-musician. A man with big ideas.

Rubinchik: His friend. An ex-wigmaker.

Perl the flour-sifter: A woman who sells flour and drones on endlessly.

Mendl the butler: Formerly a servant, now a butler.

Yokheved the maid: A house maid. A girl with self-respect.

A butcher, a grocer, Directors of the local religious school, ladies, gentlemen, simple folks.

PLACE: A Jewish town in the old country.

TIME: Before the First World War.

FIRST ACT

A spacious room, furnished as a tailor's shop. A long table covered with cloth, scissors, and tailor's chalk markers. The two young apprentices, Motl Kasoy and Kopl Falbon, sit at the table working and sighing. By the window: a sewing machine. Two doors: one to the street, the other to the kitchen.

Motl: What are you sighing about?

Kopl: What are *you* sighing about? You tell me first.

Motl: I bet I know what you're sighing about.

Kopl: If you know, why do you ask? (Pause).

Kopl: You mean Beylke. (Looks down)

Motl: Kopl, if you promise to keep your mouth shut, I'll tell you something.

Kopl: (Gives him his hand) You have my word.

Motl: (Looks around) How long are we going to beat around the bush? Why are we playing games? This isn't getting us anywhere. It's about time to talk about it — once and for all. I'll be damned if we don't both love the same girl.

Kopl: You mean Beylke? (Looks down)

Motl: Aren't you smart, old friend! Who else would I be talking about — the Rabbi's daughter? Of course I'm talking about the boss's daughter, about Beylke. So let's face it, it's either you or me — we can't both marry the same girl. So what do you say, Kopl?

Kopl: I say we can't.

Motl: Boy, are you a genius! I say let her choose. You or me. Is that clear?

Kopl: Clear as day.

Motl: That's what I call sharp. But what do we do, my dear Kopl, if she loves us both equally?

Kopl:	Right! What do we do then?
Motl:	Now you're getting to the heart of it! In that case there is only one thing we can do.
Kopl:	What, Motl?
Motl:	We'll draw lots. The one who wins will get her. Got it? (Kopl nods his head). Now then, let's pledge to keep our bargain. Let's join forces so Beylke will be ours, I mean yours or mine. Agreed? Give me your hand! (Kopl gives him his hand). Let me have your ugly face and let me kiss you, pal of mine! (They kiss noisily on the cheeks. At that moment the outside door opens and Beylke comes in with a package of muslin. She puts the package on the table, takes off her hat, straightens her hair, and is about to sit down at the sewing machine.)
Beylke:	Motl Kasoy! Kopl Falbon! Why are you standing around like bridegrooms under a canopy! Why don't you take the material. (The two young men pounce on the package. Beylke laughs.)
Motl:	Beylke! We were about to ask you something.
Kopl:	(Sighing) Yes, ask you something.
Beylke:	Both of you the same thing, or each one a different thing?
Motl:	The same thing, but from each of us separately... from both of us.
Kopl:	Really from each of us, that is.
Beylke:	(Covers her ears with her hands) Tra-ta-ta-ta-ta! If you both talk together...
Motl:	(To Kopl) Let me do the talking.
Kopl:	(To Motl) Okay, you do the talking.
Motl:	Oh Beylke! How should I say it? We've been trying to tell you for a long time.

FIRST ACT

Kopl: (Sighs) For a long time!

Motl: (To Kopl) Let me do the talking. Make up your mind— it's either me or you.

Kopl: Talk, talk! Am I stopping you?

Motl: (To Beylke) However, we wanted to talk to your father first.

Kopl: The boss, you know.

Motl: (Gives Kopl an angry look) Then we decided we should talk to you first.

Kopl: Because we don't know which one of us...

Motl: Why do you take the words out of my mouth?

Beylke: Shush! You know what? Let's draw lots. The one who wins will talk.

Motl: Long life to you! That's what we've just been saying, that we should draw lots.

Kopl: Yes, let's draw lots, but about another thing.

Beylke: What thing?

Kopl: That we... that you...

Motl: Listen to him. (Apes him) That we... that you... Let me talk.

Kopl: So talk! You talk.

Motl: So we decided... since we don't know who, I mean, whom, who, whom... so we should draw lots... the one who wins... he will, I mean, you will... Damn! It doesn't come out right.

Beylke: Ha, ha, ha.

(The door opens. Eti Meni comes in with a big basket full of vegetables. The apprentices throw themselves into their work. Beylke turns to her sewing machine.)

Eti Meni: Your father's not here yet? (Empties the basket) The price of garlic has gone sky high, God help us! Good thing that onions are cheap. But when I talk to him, he says it's got to be garlic! Here he comes, my breadwinner, speak of the Devil!

(Shimele Saroker comes in with a strange, big cap and with an old, faded, torn overcoat. The minute he comes in he throws the coat aside. He is wearing a white shirt and a vest. Tallis fringes stick out from under his shirt. The vest has big pockets and the right side is covered with needles. His beard has a white streak. A tape measure hangs around his neck. He puts on a pair of glasses and a yarmulke, which hardly shows through his thick hair. He starts working right away. He marks the garment with his tailor's chalk and cuts it.)

Shimele: (Cutting and humming a tune) Amkho, my people, cut and press. (To his wife) What were you saying about the Devil?

Eti Meni: (Brings a few pots in from the kitchen, takes a seat against the wall, and peels potatoes.) I was saying — speak of the Devil! I was talking about garlic and right away you showed up.

Shimele: (Waves the chalk) I can clearly see the parallel. That's also why ducks go barefoot and geese don't wear pants. (His daughter and the apprentices laugh.)

Eti Meni: (Offended) He preaches and they crack up! Maybe you can tell me what strikes you so funny?

Shimele: You tell me! What has garlic to do with me?

Eti Meni: Garlic costs a fortune and garlic is exactly what you want.

Shimele: (Bangs on the table) That's why you mention the Devil? Where are my scissors? (Finds the scissors) Here they are. (Cuts the material along the chalk-marks and keeps taking off the tape from around

FIRST ACT

                his neck and checking the measurements, meanwhile humming a tune. His daughter and the apprentices join in.)

Eti Meni: (Sighs) Any minute that ladies' man will come — our landlord's rent-collector. A plague on his head and on the landlord's hands and feet, and a little on his son too. (The apprentices laugh.)

Shimele: What do you have against the landlord? Is it his fault that he has an apartment and we live in it? (To the apprentices who are laughing) Why don't you get back to your irons? Any minute the landlord's son will show up to try on his suit. (The apprentices start ironing energetically.) I promised him it would be ready today, and I have to keep my word. Shimele Saroker is not one of those fly-by-night patch makers. (The door opens. Solomon Fein comes in, smooth-shaven, clean, and dressed to the nines from head to toe. Shimele Saroker welcomes him with a polite smile.) Speaking of the Devil, we were just talking about you.

Solomon: Really? Saying good things, I hope?

Eti Meni: Of course, good things! Would we say bad things about you, God forbid? What do we have against you?

Solomon: (To Eti Meni) I'm very glad to hear that. (To Shimele) And what about my summer-suit, my dear Mr. Saroker?

Shimele: Your summer-suit? I wish I had the rent money for your papa as surely as I have your summer-suit.

Eti Meni: (To her husband) Tell him he should tell his papa, and his papa should tell the rent-collector, to be good enough to stop hounding us for the rent.

Shimele: (Takes an unfinished summer-jacket off the

dummy and tries the jacket on Solomon Fein.) My life should be as perfect as this fits you! When I do a job, I see to it that it comes out perfect — no maybe about it! My luck should shine like that jacket!

Eti Meni: Amen!

Shimele: (Staring at the suit) I'd like to see you get such a piece of work in the finest clothing store, as true as I'm a Jew!

Eti Meni: Amen!

Shimele: (To his wife) Praised be His name and let us say Amen. Are you in a synagogue or something that you keep saying Amen?

Solomon: When will it be ready?

Shimele: When will it be ready? I wish I would be ready with the rent money I owe your father as fast as I'll be ready with this suit. But your rent-collector hounds me. Say — how about having a word with your papa, and asking him to . . .

Solomon: (Interrupts him) That's none of my business.

Shimele: (To his wife) He says he doesn't get involved in his father's business.

Solomon: (Speaking to Shimele and Eti Meni, but looking constantly at Beylke). Good-bye.

Shimele: (Accompanies him to the door and bows) Good-bye. My regards to your papa. Tell him he shouldn't worry — with God's help I'll probably be able to pay him soon.

Eti Meni: (Yells after him) And thank him, too.

Shimele: (Standing at the door with his head down) It's none of his business — ha! (Everybody works in an uneasy silence.)

Eti Meni: (Peeling potatoes) Fat chance he'll put in a good

FIRST ACT

	word about us to his father!
Motl:	(Ironing) The apple doesn't fall far from the tree.
Kopl:	(Spits on his finger and on the iron) Once a bourgeois, always a bourgeois.
Shimele:	(Puts away the scissors and speaks to the apprentices) Bourgeois? I'd love to see what you wise guys would do if your father was Mr. Osher Fein. Would you be any better? Talk, talk, talk. Bourgeois! God help me! (To his wife) And you also indulge in "social criticism," Peti Meti? (Looks into the pot) It seems to me that you are doing important work peeling potatoes, so peel! Don't you know any other dishes besides potatoes? (Sings) Sunday potatoes, Monday potatoes, Tuesday potatoes...
Eti Meni:	Look at him! Maybe roast squab and marzipan would be more to your refined taste? (Stops peeling, but cuts the potatoes into small pieces and transfers them from one pot to another)
Shimele:	Why not? With God's help we could eat roast squab and marzipan this very day. Today is May second — today we will know. (Looks at the clock on the wall) It will soon be ten o'clock. I should send someone to find out how much I won.
Eti Meni:	Ha, ha! How much you won? Listen to him! You should find out first if you won anything at all, and then see how much.
Shimele:	(Gives her a dirty look) Is that so, smarty? For your information, I can save myself the trouble. My ticket won — that much I know!
Eti Meni:	What makes you so sure? Did somebody write you a letter?
Shimele:	(Gives her a contemptuous look through his glasses as if to imply that he had some secret

information) If you knew what kind of dream I had last night, you would stop making wisecracks. But what's the use of talking to you? (Unbuttons his vest, opens up an inside pocket, and takes out a shawl inside of which a torn, crushed piece of yellow paper is wrapped) In a minute you will hear the dream, Shimele's dream. (Everyone puts away his work and prepares to hear about Shimele's dream.) I hate empty dreams! When Shimele dreams a dream, there is something to listen to, by God! (Takes off his glasses) I dreamt, listen to this, that I was standing by my table, just as you see me now, with my iron and scissors, and I was cutting a piece of work, a Prince Albert coat made of very expensive cloth. As I stood there, preoccupied, with my scissors in my hand, I happened to look up and I saw a tree in the middle of the room.

Beylke: A tree in the middle of the room?

Shimele: And on the tree grew golden coins.

Beylke: On the tree grew golden coins?

Shimele: Golden coins. I called your mother: "Eti Meni," I said, "do you see the golden coins?" She said, "I do." I said, "So why don't you say something?" And she said, "What do you want me to say?" I said to her: "Forgive me for the inconvenience, but would you mind climbing up the tree and giving it a good shake? I will collect the fallen coins." She said, "You climb. Why should I climb?" I said, "What are you afraid of? That you're going to lose something?" And she answered, "My enemies should lose an arm and a leg."

Eti Meni: It's a lie! I never said that!

Shimele: (To his wife) Dummy! It was just a dream. (To his daughter) Here is the receipt. When you finish

FIRST ACT

	the piece of work on your sewing machine, be so good as to go to the bank. Do you know where it is?
Beylke:	(Continuing to work) It's in the trade center.
Shimele:	Exactly... and show them the ticket... don't give it to them, just show it... and ask how much I won.
Eti Meni:	(Continuing to work) Again how much? You're a comedian!
Shimele:	(Angry) What a world we live in! Look who is an expert on comedy! I dream a dream, and she talks to me about comedy! She thinks I woke up in the morning just like that and started making up stories out of the blue. True I am only a tailor, but I have as much intelligence to win the jackpot as the biggest millionaire. It's a good trick just to hold on to a lottery ticket for some twenty years, starving for a few pennies but never selling it — only Shimele Saroker could do that, by God! (Keeps ironing, humming. To his daughter) Finished? Now you can go. (Gives her the receipt carefully) Don't lose it, God forbid! It's money — a lot of it. (Beylke exits)
Eti Meni:	Shimon! How much is it?
Shimele:	What?
Eti Meni:	This jackpot you're talking about.
Shimele:	(Looks at her) And if I tell you, will you know? Two times one hundred thousand.
Eti Meni:	(Shocked) Two time a thousand and a hundred?
Shimele:	Not two times a thousand and a hundred — two times a hundred thousand. Women, women! Just to describe them is a comedy.
Eti Meni:	Is that so? So I'm a comedy in your opinion?
Shimele:	Who else? Me?

(The door opens. Koltun the rent-collector comes in. He is a dark-haired young man, somewhat stooped, wearing clothes that are new, but hang on him like a sack. When he talks, he keeps smiling and pulling up his long sleeves. Talks hastily and with a lisp. He tries to cover his balding head with the few remaining shiny black hairs. He is always in a sweat.)

Shimele: (To the new arrival) Speak of the Devil! We were just talking about you.

Koltun: Good things, I hope. Ha, ha! (Walks around)

Eti Meni: Good things, of course, Why should we say bad things?

Shimele: (Shows him a chair) Have a seat, Mr. Koltun.

Koltun: Thank you. I didn't come here to sit. Ha, ha! I came on business. (Looks around searching for something) You probably know already what I came for.

Eti Meni: (Observes his searching looks) I wish we didn't. What are you looking for, last year's snow?

Koltun: (Ignoring her) Today is already May second. Ha, ha!

Shimele: (Putting a thread in his needle) I know very well that today is May second, because yesterday was the drawing for the lottery. (Looks at his watch)

Koltun: What drawing? (Puffs on his cigar)

Shimele: (Coughs) How much did you pay for that piece of rope, Mr. Koltun?

Koltun: First of all, don't call me Mr. Koltun. Ha, ha! Call me by my real name, Yefim Pantelemonovich — that's what everyone calls me.

Shimele: My apologies, Yefim Pantalonovich.

Koltun: Not Pantalonovich, but Pantelemonovich.

Shimele: Let it be Pantelemonovich. Do you believe in dreams? Yes or no?

FIRST ACT

Koltun: Why not? For example, I had a dream that they extracted my wisdom tooth, and, in fact, a sister of mine died right at that time. How come we're talking about dreams? (Looks around) Where is your daughter? How come she isn't around? (The apprentices exchange looks.)

Shimele: My Beylke? She'll be back any minute. (Sighs) If God wills it, today I will become a rich man, with a hatful of gold — cut and press!

Koltun: You know, that wouldn't be a bad idea — in fact it would be (ha ha ha) a very, very good idea!

Shimele: (Looks at him) What would be so good about it?

Koltun: It would save me, ha ha, the waiting for your rent money, week after week and month after month. But tell me, where will you get so much money all of a sudden? Did a rich uncle of yours die in America? Or what?

Shimele: No. (Stops working) No! My uncle in America is alive and in good health. (Glances at the clock on the wall) We'll know in just half an hour. I have a lottery ticket, you see.

Koltun: (Surprised) You have lottery tickets? But when it comes to rent money...

Eti Meni: Tickets? Who is talking about tickets? Just one ticket. And even that one has been guarded like a treasure since Methuselah's time. My enemies should get what that ticket will bring in!

Shimele: And in spite of all that, that lone ticket can win the jackpot — the future is nobody's private property.

Koltun: (Stands up) If you mean to tell me that that's how you're going to pay the rent, you are making a big mistake, my dear tailor. Lottery tickets don't win. It's a lot of nonsense. It's only the bank's gimmick to get money out of people . You see

	that ceiling? That ceiling will fall and strike you before you will win the jackpot.
Eti Meni:	A thunderbolt should strike my enemies! Listen to the man talk!
Koltun:	Listen, woman, it's only an example. My bosses have a few more lottery tickets than you have, but not one of them has ever won. Forget about such things! You'd do better to look for some other way to get the rent money, because I must tell you, regretfully (Looks at his watch) that in half an hour I'll be back with the marshal to evict you from the apartment. (The words strike like thunder. Everybody trembles and is paralyzed. Nobody can say a word, except Eti Meni.)
Eti Meni:	(Stands up, goes over to Koltun) Evict us? With the marshal? What do you mean evict us? And with the marshal yet? Don't we count for anything? Shimon! Why do you take it from him? I can go to the Feins, too. I'll ask them if it's really right to evict people who've been tenants for so many years. I will!
Koltun:	(Hands in his pockets) Don't get worked up, my dear woman. The Feins that you mention have nothing to do with it. I'm the one who swore out the complaint, and I am bringing the marshal, and I am evicting you from the apartment if you don't pay me for at least three months.
Shimele:	Is that so? So that's what you really are? In that case you can go to Hell, as true as I'm a Jew! Out! (Takes him by the collar and throws him out)

(A sound of banging and people talking. Shmuel Yossi the butcher, a big guy with a kerchief around his neck, comes in, followed by Moyshe Velvl the grocer, smeared with herring, followed in turn by Perl the flour-sifter, covered with flour from head to toe.)

FIRST ACT

Shmuel: Who gave the bastard such a kick? He almost knocked us over! Good thing I shoved him away so hard I knocked his teeth out.

Shimele: I just showed him the way to the door. Take a seat, Reb Yossi. Sit down, Moyshe Velvl! So what's new in the world?

Shmuel: Thank you for inviting us to sit, but we have no time to sit. We came for money. You must know, my dear tailor, that I always gave you meat, not bones.

Moyshe: And I gave you groceries...

Eti Meni: Sit down, Perl. Why don't you sit?

Perl: Thank you. I've sat long enough. You think I'd come just for my pleasure? My enemies and your enemies and all our enemies should have as much time to spend on eating a piece of bread as I have time to leave my dough and my flour and go ask for repayment of old, old debts, because I have nobody, not even to leave the shop with, in case the Devil should come to play his evil tricks, because my son spends his time with books, day and night, books and books and more books, and my daughter is in the house. House? You call that a house? What house? It's a hovel, not a house! Meanwhile I see Moyshe Velvl the grocer go by. "Good morning. Where are you going?" He says: "To the tailor, to Shimele Saroker, to get money." I ask him: "Money? He has money now, does he?" And he says: "Yes..."

Eti Meni: (To the grocer) What are you talking about?

Moyshe: The story goes like this: the matchmaker, Soloveitchik...

Perl: (Doesn't let him talk) If this is true, I think to myself I have to go too, because the money they owe me is not for tobacco or diamonds. They owe me money for flour, and flour is the most necessary of all necessities. See, here is a bread. (She sees a half-loaf of bread on the shelf, stands up and takes it.) This bread was made with my flour, my blood, my life. What else do I have besides this bit of flour? If everybody came and took my flour on credit, what would become of me? Huh? Where would I get the money to pay for my flour? Huh? Who would provide for my children, huh?

Eti Meni: Shush, quiet! Let someone else say a word. (To Moyshe Velvl) What did Soloveitchik say to you?

Moyshe Velvl: He told me that he has money for you.

Shimele: What the hell is going on?

Eti Meni: My troubles should fall on his head.

Perl: Are you telling me I'm crazy?

(The door opens. Soloveitchik the matchmaker comes in. He wears a fashionable bowler hat. He is elaborately dressed, but everything — hat, jacket, trousers, boots — is either torn or fits badly.)

Shimele: Welcome, Mr. Matchmaker! Speaking of the Devil, we've just been talking about you.

Soloveitchik: Nothing bad, I hope.

Eti Meni: Bad, good. Why have you spread the story all over town that you have money for us?

Soloveitchik: (Gestures with his hands) This much money! You can't even imagine — it's just extraordinary!

Shimele: You mean you have a match for my daughter. I know you very well by now. (The apprentices look at each other, begin ironing, and sigh heavily.)

Soloveitchik: What a question! You call it just a match? It's

FIRST ACT

something extraordinary! I should live so long, and you and your wife too, that I'm not just blowing smoke! When I tell you what this is all about, you'll grab it with both hands. There's only one problem — there are too many people here. (To the visitors) Excuse us, ladies and gentlemen. (The butcher and the grocer step back. Perl doesn't move from her seat. Soloveitchik goes over to her.) Excuse me, Madame! (She does not move.)

Perl: What do you mean excuse me? What's this Madame business? You say you've brought money for the tailor? So where is your money? He owes me money for flour, not for diamonds. This bread that you see was baked with my flour, my blood, my life.

Soloveitchik: (Pushes away the flour-woman, who keeps talking) A veritable plague, this flour-woman — she's really outrageous. (To Shimele) The bridegroom I am proposing for your daughter is a man of independent means. He has an excellent job. He is in complete charge of a house. In a word, you know him very well. It's the superintendent of this house, Koltun. (The apprentices become agitated and drop the work.)

Shimele: (Jumps in anger) You mean this Yefim Pantalonovich? The scoundrel I just kicked out through that door? By God!

Beylke: (Runs in, red-faced, can hardly talk) Father, it's good news!

Shimele: What? How much?

Beylke: The grand prize! The jackpot!

Eti Meni: (Claps her hands) My God!

Perl: Now what? Some new misfortune? Woe is me!

Shimele: (Beside himself.) Eti Meni? Do you hear? People!

Congratulate me! My ticket won! Won! The grand prize! The jackpot! (Starts running around the house)

Perl: Let me go! Let me go! Where?

Soloveitchik: (Pushes Perl away) Excuse me Madame! (Tries to say something, but is unable to speak. The others are also speechless, astonished. Motl and Kopl have slunk off to a corner, and are standing there, silent and troubled.)

Beylke: (Still wearing her hat, excited) The whole city knows about it already. The director of the bank, the bookkeeper, the Feins — all of them are coming here soon.

Eti Meni: (Claps her hands together) All of them coming here? My God! (Flustered, she sits down on a chair and wipes the sweat from her face with her apron.)

(Himmelfarb, the bookkeeper, and Goldenthaler, the director of the bank, come in.)

Himmelfarb: Who is the tailor here?

Shimele: (Steps forward proudly) The tailor — that's me!

Himmelfarb: (Looks at the amazed faces around him. To the tailor) Have you heard the news? Your ticket, which is now in our bank, has won the jackpot! Our bank, the Bank of Commerce, is the luckiest bank in the world. This is the fourth time we have a winning ticket in our bank. Anyone who buys a ticket in our bank stands a chance of winning. Here is the director of the bank, Mr. Goldenthaler. You can ask him.

Goldenthaler: You are *the* Mr. Saroker? You must have heard it by now? (Shakes his hand) Mazel tov! Congratulations!

FIRST ACT

Perl: (To the banker and the others) Good people, please tell me! What happened? Why the mazel tov? Who gave birth? Or is it a wedding? Or an engagement? What?

Soloveitchik: (Pushes Perl away) Excuse me, Madame! (Shakes hands with Shimele) Mazel tov! (Hugs and kisses him)

Koltun: (Comes running — confused) Huh? What? Is it true? What did I tell you? What did you have to worry about? You can stay here and stay and stay as long as you want. Look, the landlord himself is here!

(Mr. Osher Fein and his son come in. Koltun steps aside and remains silent.)

Osher Fein: (Shakes hands with the bank director, but with no one else. Says a few words to him, and then turns to the tailor.) Congratulations, Mr. Saroker! I am very pleased, very pleased that your good fortune happened in my house. (Solomon comes over. To his son) You hear? It's really true!

Solomon: How much? Two hundred thousand? Congratulations! (His eyes glitter. He looks at the tailor and catches Beylke's eye) I am very happy for you, very happy, Mademoiselle Sorokin.

Beylke: (Still red-faced, smiling) First of all, it's Saroker, not Sorokin. Second, what's it to you?

Solomon: Because, you understand... (Stops talking as the two apprentices look at him intensely. The young men move away and talk quietly to one another.)

Motl: Well, Kopl, what do you say now?

Kopl: What should I say.? It's fate! A man suddenly becomes a... a bourgeois! A millionaire!

Motl: I'm happy for them with all my heart, but what will happen to us now?

Kopl: What would you like to happen?

Motl: (Looks at him for a moment) You're an idiot!

Osher Fein (To the tailor) Do you need money by any chance? (Puts his hand in his pocket)

Himmelfarb: (Leaps forward) No! Money? Allow me! Money you'll find in our bank. (To the tailor) You have an account in our bank, a cash account! (Looks at the bank director)

Shmuel Yossi: (To Eti Meni) So how much meat should I send you?

Moyshe Velvl: As they say: When God gives with a spoon, people give with a bucket.

Perl: (Hearing people speak of money, pushes her way up to Mr. Fein and then to the bank director) Is that so? People are paying money? How about paying me? I am a widow. They owe me for flour, and flour is the first necessity. (Counts on her fingers) A ruble twenty for dark flour, 65 kopikes more for rye flour, and 65 kopikes more, and another 65 . . .

Soloveitchik: (Pulls her away) Excuse me, Madame! (Sees Solomon standing at Beylke's side and says to the tailor) Listen here! I have an idea for you, a brand new idea, a great idea, I swear.

Shimele: (Runs around like a madman, from one person to another. Yells above the hubbub) Just you wait and see! I'll show you, I'll show everyone who Shimele Saroker is and what Shimele Saroker can do, by God! (To his wife) So, Eti Meni, what do you say about my dream now?

Eti Meni: Of course! After all, you're not some child.

Shimele: (Takes off his glasses. To his daughter) My child! (Cries for joy) (Curtain falls slowly.)

SECOND ACT

A large room, looks like a furniture store. Any furniture you think of can be found here. Everything is new and shiny. The master of the house, Shimele Saroker, is wearing new and elegant clothes: a brand-new silk dressing gown, a multicolored velvet vest with golden buttons. Everything is new and freshly ironed. The shirt shines. The beard is thoroughly trimmed. Golden spectacles. No yarmulke. Hardly any similarity to the former tailor. His wife, Eti Meni, is covered from head to toe with beautifully embroidered silk and velvet. There are pearls around her neck and big diamond earrings in her ears. All eight fingers have shiny rings on them. Shimele is holding a book, and is rocking in his chair and reading, seemingly with great interest. She sits idle, glaring at her jewelry.

Eti Meni: (In a sing-song voice) Shimon! Shimon! (He doesn't hear her. (Again, with the same sing-song. This time louder) Shimon! Shimon!

Shimele: (Tearing himself away from his book, then imitating her) Shimon! Shimon? Semyon Makarovich, not Shimon!

Eti Meni: Semyon Makarovich, what's the time on your golden watch?

Shimele: Quarter to eleven. Why do you ask?

Eti Meni: No reason. Just like that. Three weeks ago at this time we didn't know that our ticket would win the jackpot. (She cracks each knuckle in turn, then surveys her ringed fingers. A pause.) Shimon! Shimon?

Shimele: (Looking at her) Once again Shimon? Bird-brain! How many times a day must it be banged into your head: Semyon Makarovich! Semyon Makarovich! Semyon Makarovich!

Eti Meni: I hope you don't mind my asking, Semyon Makarovich, but what are you doing there?

Shimele: You can see for yourself what I'm doing. I'm reading. (Can't tear himself away from the book.)

Eti Meni: I can see that you're reading. I mean what are you reading?

Shimele: And if I tell you, will you know? I'm reading a story, that's what I'm reading.

Eti Meni: What kind of a story?

Shimele: Actually it's not a story, it's a description... a... a... satire — and leave me alone. (Rocks in his chair, keeps reading)

Eti Meni: It looks like you got up on the wrong side of the bed. (Pause) Since you're all steamed up, I'm afraid you're reading without understanding what you're reading.

Shimele: (Goes on rocking in his chair) For your information, it so happens that I do understand what I'm reading. I'm reading a satire by some joker who makes fun of the whole world. His name is Sholem Aleichem.

Eti Meni: Hasn't he anything better to do? What has he got against the world?

Shimele: Nothing. He just describes some tailor who was a pauper among paupers and overnight became a rich man.

Eti Meni: None of his business! Well, what else?

Shimele: Nothing else. He makes fun of him and his wife. A real son of a gun! My kind of guy!

Eti Meni: My troubles should be on his head! What has he got against the wife?

Shimele: He makes fun of both of them, but he makes the wife out to be a real nincompoop — the Devil take him!

Eti Meni: Amen! (Spits) I wouldn't touch such a crab with a

SECOND ACT 41

	ten-foot pole. Besides, what kind of an occupation is that for a Jew, to sit down just like that to read a book and rock back and forth, like on the Sabbath after the meal?
Shimele:	What can I do? I'm going out of my mind. I need something to do — I was used to working, as sure as I can stitch a seam!
Eti Meni:	You've worked enough. Let your enemies work instead of you. (Pause) Shimon! (Spits) I mean Semyon Makarovich! Where are we going tonight?
Shimele:	Would you like to go to the theater?
Eti Meni:	The theater? (Yawns) Boring. I don't understand a word. If only they would play in Yiddish! I'd rather go to the movies — at least they don't talk.
Shimele:	You mean to the cinema? Just wait. As soon as I sign the contract with the film company, we'll go every night without paying a cent.
Eti Meni:	(Cautious) You promise not to get mad? I want to tell you something.
Shimele:	Me mad? When do I get mad? As long as you make sense, you can tell me anything you want.
Eti Meni:	I don't like the business with those two con men you hang out with.
Shimele:	What makes you think they're con men? Do you know them?
Eti Meni:	It's just *because* I don't know them. That's why I'm afraid they'll con you.
Shimele:	Me? Con *me?* Nonsense. No one can con me! I'm signing a good contract with them. I'll nail them down real good. I've got 22 paragraphs in this contract, as sure as I know my name!

Eti Meni: 22 paragraphs? They'll come up with a twenty-third paragraph and snatch the money right out from under your nose.

Shimele: (Angry now) Bite your tongue! Dummy! What are you talking about? Do you hear what you're saying?

Eti Meni: That's the trouble with you. Nobody can talk to you — right away you get mad.

Shimele: (Pounds his hand on the table) Peti Meti! Don't get me worked up! (Stands up and paces back and forth) You forget who you're talking to. You think you're talking to Shimele the tailor. You forget that I'm not just anybody. No more little guy! I am now Semyon Makarovich Saroker, one of the richest, if not *the* richest man in town! (Calming down) Open your ears and you'll hear what people say about me... not to mention the people who want my company... and the business propositions I keep getting... our people should see half of it!

Eti Meni: For me you're still the same as you were.

Shimele: That's the whole problem. You could at least have a little more respect.

Eti Meni: Wait, I'll take off my hat.

Shimele: (Dismisses her with a wave of his hand) What's the use talking? Where is Beylke — I mean Isabellitchke?

Eti Meni: What do you need Beylke — I mean Isabellitchke — for?

Shimele: I want her to read the mail for me, that's what I want.

Eti Meni: Again the mail? Did you get mail again?

Shimele: Mostly trash! (Points to a pile of unopened letters on the table)

SECOND ACT

Eti Meni: Very important mail! Probably from a Jew expelled from a village with his wife and children, or from a widow whose husband hanged himself because of her, or maybe even from a girl who wants to get married but has no dowry.

Shimele: Well, it's really a shame about that girl, don't you think?

Eti Meni: So you have to provide for the entire world?

Shimele: I'll do what's in my power.

Eti Meni: Is that why the good Lord gave you the grand prize?

Shimele: What else? So we could eat kasha and chicken soup?

Eti Meni: How long will you be able to provide for them?

Shimele: (Gently) Silly! The business with the film company will provide for everything. The whole town envies me. They say it could amount to half a million. But what do you know about millions!

Eti Meni: Thank God *you* know all about it, because you grew up with millions.

Shimele: All the same, here I am. (Sits down again in his chair, rocks, and reads the same book. A moment of silence.) Eti Meni! (Louder) Eti Meni!

Eti Meni: What is this Eti Meni! He wants to be called Semyon Makarovich and I should be (Imitates him) "Eti Meni! Eti Meni!"

Shimele: (Admits he's wrong) You're right! Don't get upset — I completely forgot that your name nowadays is Ernestina Yefimevna.

Eti Meni: And you go around saying that *I'm* a bird-brain?

Shimele: You're right! I beg your pardon. You know what I wanted to ask you for, Ernestina Yefimevna?

Eti Meni: What is it you wanted to ask me for, Semyon Makarovich?

Shimele: (Begging) Some preserves.

Eti Meni: Just like that? Preserves? (Loud) Maid! Maid! (A side door opens. Yokheved the maid comes in.)

Yokheved: You called me?

Eti Meni: No, I was calling for the rabbi!

Yokheved: You couldn't call me by any other name than "maid?"

Eti Meni: And if I call you maid — why should that bother you so? Is there anything wrong with being a maid? (Gives her the keys) Here! Go get a bowl and bring some preserves for the master from the open jar, the one tied up with cloth.

Yokheved: (Takes the keys) How much should I bring?

Eti Meni: You say you've worked for rich people — you should know how much preserves a rich man eats.

Yokheved: There are all kinds of rich people. There are rich people who eat food with the tip of their knife, like a bird, and there are others, if you don't mind my saying so, who eat like pigs. No matter how much they eat, it's not enough.

Eti Meni: The worms should eat *you!* You're pretty fresh for a maid.

Yokheved: (Starts to leave with the keys. Stops for a second and says to Shimele) My name is Yokheved.

Eti Meni: Yokheved? Good thing you told me. Go to Hell, Yokheved! (Yokheved leaves. To her husband) What a fresh maid! (Loud) Mendl! Mendl! (Mendl the butler enters in a tuxedo with a white bowtie and a high collar. His lips are fat and dark. He keeps his head cocked to one side. His hands hang loosely by his sides, like unnecessary appendages.)

SECOND ACT

Mendl: Did you call me?

Eti Meni: Who else would I call, the rabbi's wife? I sent the maid for some preserves. Go see to it that she doesn't take too much for herself, like a hungry cat eating cream.

Mendl: (Starts to go, but turns back and says to Shimele) Sir, the big-shots are waiting in the hall.

Shimele: What big-shots?

Mendl: Those two guys from the theater.

Shimele: (Puts the book aside) What? You mean Vigdorchuk and Rubinchik? My partners in the film company? Why don't they come in?

Mendl: (With a smile) Because I'm making them wait.

Shimele: What do mean you're making them wait?

Mendl: (Quite seriously) That's the custom with rich people. When a visitor comes and he is poorly dressed, I take him by the neck and throw him out of the house. Now if he is well dressed, I have to announce him to the master first, and only then, only if the master tells me to, I let him in.

Shimele: (Amazed. To his wife) Ernestina Yefimevna. What do you say to that? Isn't that something?

Eti Meni: (To her husband) Big deal! You've got nothing better to do than to chatter with a butler in the middle of everything, and in the meantime the maid will gobble up the whole jar of preserves. (To the butler) Go do as you're told!

Mendl: (On the way out. Stops) So what shall I tell them?

Shimele: Tell whom?

Mendl: The big-shots.

Shimele: Nothing. Send them in. (Mendl the butler leaves. At the door he bumps into Yokheved the maid, puts a finger into the preserves and licks it. Yokheved slaps his hand away and brings the preserves to Shimele. She starts to leave, but stands there for a moment.)

Yokheved: (To Eti Meni) Anything else?

Eti Meni: What else?

Yokheved: (Pause) When you need to call me next time, you should know that my name is Yokheved. (Exits)

Eti Meni: (To Shimele) What's this? She's like God's punishment to us, not like a maid. (The door opens. Mendl lets Vigdorchuk and Rubinchik in. The two men are very expensively dressed and shaved like artists, carrying top-hats and wearing gloves and expensive ties.)

Shimele: (Stands up, very polite) Welcome, my dear guests. Did you bring along the revised contract? (To his wife) Ernestina Yefimevna, tell the maid to bring more preserves and a little brandy, too. (Eti Meni gets up unenthusiastically and goes to the kitchen herself for the preserves and brandy. Shimele to the young men) Let's have a look at that contract. (Vigdorchuk takes out a paper with writing on it.) That is, my daughter will look it over, I, unfortunately, am a little weak when it comes to reading. God gave me a daughter with a sharp mind. You know her — she is, so to speak, my bookkeeper, my lawyer, and my secretary, you name it, all in one. She can read and write and handle figures like nobody's business! (Offers them cigarettes in a silver box) Mr. Rubinchik, Mr. Vigdorchuk! Go ahead, try these cigarettes! These are what I call cigarettes — really good stuff! (The two stand up and take cigarettes with thumb and forefinger.) That's it. So where do we stand in this matter? Tell me, please, my dear Vigdorchuk, my dear Rubinchik, how should I

SECOND ACT

	put it, how did two young men like yourselves — I hope you don't mind my asking — how did you get into such a lucrative business as the film business?
Vigdorchuk:	Well, it's a long story...
Rubinchik:	I could sum it up in a few words. We are, as you can see...
Vigdorchuk:	(Doesn't let him speak) Let me talk. I'll wrap it up in three words. I and my friend Rubinchik are men with big ideas...
Rubinchik:	With big plans.
Vigdorchuk:	We have always been men of the theater. I, for example, was a musician, and a famous one to boot. I played in all the theaters. And my friend Rubinchik is also not just some guy off the street. He had a wig-making business, and he used to go to theaters and do the makeup for the actors. I've got to give him this, the son of a gun — when he puts makeup on somebody, it's like real. Then something happened: times got bad, so I became an actor in the film business. I worked one night, two nights, three nights, and then I started to think about the whole thing: What's the trick to this whole film business, I asked myself? It turns out that there's no trick to it at all! I found out that the trick is no trick.
Rubinchik:	It's a joke!
Vigdorchuk:	(Corrects himself) I mean the trick is a pretty tricky one, but it's nothing much. For those who understand it, it's no trick at all, it's a trifle.
Rubinchik:	Zero plus nothing.
Shimele:	I don't understand. I'm a simple man. One or the other, either milkhik or fleyshik, either here or there. According to you, first it's a big thing and

	then it's nothing at all, a joke. You've got me all confused.
Vigdorchuk:	(To Rubinchik) It's all your fault, because you keep interrupting me. I'll explain the whole thing very simply.
Rubinchik:	Be my guest, go ahead and explain.
Shimele:	Now you have to understand that my wife and I are great movie fans. Even when I was — knock on wood — a simple tailor, we went to the movies every week if we had a few pennies. Now, since God gave us the grand prize, we spend almost every single night in the movies. So we would like very much to know, especially now that we're talking about investing money, the... the... essence (Snapping his fingers), the trick to it all. There must be some kind of trick to it... something... (Snaps again) Some clever little twist.
Vigdorchuk:	Of course there's a trick to it!
Rubinchik:	You can bet on that!
Vigdorchuk:	(Cuts him off) Allow me, please. I will explain the whole thing exactly. (Moves closer to the tailor) You're a smart fellow — the thing is very simple. Have you noticed that in the balcony facing the screen there is a lamp with a wheel? On that wheel, which keeps turning, there's a strip of celluloid, a long strip. (Gestures with his hands)
Rubinchik:	(Reads his friend's lips, nods his head in agreement) That's the film.
Vigdorchuk:	On the film are all the pictures that you see on the screen. Are you with me so far?
Shimele:	Bear with me, would you wait a minute? I want, you understand, I want my wife to be here too and hear your explanation. (Turns to his wife who

SECOND ACT

comes in from the other room. She is followed by Mendl the butler carrying a tray. On the tray is a pitcher with liquor and glasses. Yokheved comes behind him, also with a tray. The servants put the trays on the table and exit.)

Eti Meni: Here is some brandy and preserves. You can take some if you like ...

Shimele: They'll take, God willing, you bet they will! (Fills the glasses. Turns to his wife) Do you want to hear the trick behind the movies — how it is that it turns and we see on the screen everything that is happening in the world? Sit down and you'll hear something. You love the movies so much — you could spend your days and nights there.

Eti Meni: And you, of course, hate them. (Sits down on a soft cushion, leans on a silk pillow with multicolor fringes, and rests her hands so all her rings are displayed.) All right. Let's hear.

Vigdorchuk: (Tries to face Eti Meni while addressing Shimele) So where were we?

Rubinchik: We were talking about the film. How the wheel turns and the lamp ...

Shimele: (To his wife) In the balcony, facing the screen, you saw a lantern, didn't you? There's a wheel there that keeps turning. (Shows with his hands how it turns. Picks up the pitcher and fills three glasses. To the guests) Let it turn. In the meantime we'll have something to wet our whistles. Lekhayim! May God bless us all, Amen! (Drinks. The guests sip the liquor.) Now, go on, shoot!

Vigdorchuk: Now then, the whole thing in a nutshell.(Gestures with his hands) Here you have a piece of cloth ...

Rubinchik: An ordinary piece of cloth ...

Vigdorchuk: There is nothing on the cloth ...

Rubinchik: Absolutely nothing...

Vigdorchuk: And on the other side of the cloth there is also nothing...

Rubinchik: Absolutely nothing. (Shimele looks at his wife in surprise.)

Eti Meni: Who are you kidding? What do you mean there's nothing there? You think we never go to the movies? It sure costs us enough money! And you mean to tell me that there's nothing on the other side of this screen! You take us for little children or something? You think we buy your fairy tales?

Vigdorchuk: (Confused, smiling) Don't get so upset, Madame — we are professionals. We work in the movies day and night. It's our whole life.

Rubinchik: Our livelihood.

Shimele: (To Vigdorchuk) Well, go on, shoot! Make it short!

Vigdorchuk: So, there is nothing on the screen. The main thing is the wheel, across the room by the lamp (Turns and points with his hand at the door. They all turn their heads to the door.) Over there, where the strip keeps turning.

Rubinchik: It's called the film. (The door opens, and just then the following scene unfolds: Several of the Directors of the local religious school try to push themselves into the room, but Mendl blocks them with both hands.)

Mendl: Wait a minute. Wait till I announce you.

Directors: (In unison) What do you mean, announce us? What's this announcement business? We need a contribution for the local religious school.

Shimele: (Shouts to Mendl) You fool — may the Devil take you! What have you got against those gentlemen? Let them in! (Mendl moves aside, but

SECOND ACT

motions with his hand that they should take off their hats. They hesitate about taking them off — some do, some don't. They step forward slowly.)

Eti Meni: (To the Directors) What is it you have to say?

Shimele: Sit down. You can keep your hats on. We're not Gentiles yet — we're still Jews. (The Directors gain confidence and sit down.)

1st Director: We've come to you, Reb Shimon, because we've heard that since God gave you his help you keep giving away money. We are the Directors of the local religious school, and we need a charitable contribution.

Eti Meni: (Puts her hand in her pocket) So why the long introduction? You say you want charity? I'll give you charity. Do you have change?

Directors: (Happy. In unison) For what?

Eti Meni: (Takes out a coin) For forty rubles. (The Directors are surprised. They look at each other and remain speechless.)

Shimele: (Jumps up, turns all colors, wants to yell at his wife, but controls himself and laughs. To the Directors) My wife wasn't listening very carefully, ha ha. She didn't realize that you are the Directors of the local religious school. She thought it was just a contribution for a person... Come, I'll give you. (Takes out a little key from his vest pocket, goes over to the safe, stands there a while, takes out a packet of four 25-ruble notes, and brings it to the Directors.) Here. Here is my contribution and write down my name in the book, my real Jewish name: Shimon, son of Reb Mayer Saroker, gives the local religious school a hundred rubles. (The Directors stand up, surprised. They thank him.)

1st Director: Reb Shimon! We say the blessing of thanks:

shehekhiyanu vekiymanu vehegianu lazman hazeh. Since our school has been a school, this is our first hundred-ruble contribution. May God give you a hundred years of happiness, success, and all the best — Amen!

The Directors: All blessings and success! Brokhe un hatzlokhe! (Say goodbye. Leave. The mood is downbeat. Eti Meni feels happy but Shimele feels sad. He paces back and forth, then stops.)

Shimele: (To himself) Yes, yes. A terrific trick! What people can come up with! Celluloid strips, screens, film . . . and the whole thing comes alive! Moves! God's wonder! (To the young men) So where were we? Yes. Let's keep track. There's one more thing my wife absolutely insists on. (To Eti Meni) Ernestina Yefimevna! I want the contract to mention explicitly that you and I and our friends have the right to go to any movie theater we want, anytime we want, day or night, free of charge.

Eti Meni: (Wringing her hands) You mean to say it's not in the contract yet?

Vigdorchuk: We forgot to put it in.

Rubinchik: Madame, our word is our bond.

Eti Meni: (Turns her anger on him) That's what you say! And when it comes to an argument, you'll say you never heard of it. We know your kind. We weren't born yesterday.

Shimele: You say we should include it? I say the same thing — include it. (Pointing to the table to Vigdorchuk) Roll up your sleeves, please, and write.

Vigdorchuk: (Writes, then reads) "We, the undersigned, add an additional point of agreement. Mr. Saroker, Madam Saroker, and any member of their family

SECOND ACT

	hereby have the right, by day or night, to enter any of our movie theaters free of charge." Satisfied?
Eti Meni:	I want them to mention my sister Feygl in the contract, too.
Vigdorchuk:	Madame, it says explicitly the Saroker family.
Eti Meni:	Her family name is not Saroker — it's Vishkrobenko.
Rubinchik:	The Madame is right.
Shimele:	In that case, add all friends and acquaintances.
Eti Meni:	Acquaintances? That's all we need! A thunderbolt should strike them! They can pay.
Rubinchik:	The Madame is absolutely right. (To his partner) Write down Madame Vishkrobenko and her children ...
Eti Meni:	No! Her, yes — the children, no. She has children — may the Devil take them! One is worse than the next.
Rubinchik:	Madame is absolutely right. Write down Madame Vishkrobenko and let that be the end of it.
Eti Meni:	What kind of Madame? Where Madame? She's a pauper, a penniless, pitiful creature. (Enter Beylke, dressed in simple clothes as always.)
Shimele:	Good thing you're here. Come read the contract for me. See if everything we agreed on is in it. (The two young men stand up to greet Beylke, give her the contract, and sit down.)
Beylke:	Can I first read it for myself? (Takes a chair. Sits and reads)
Shimele:	(To the young men, quietly) She's a smart girl — she can read Yiddish and Russian and German and anything you want. (Mendl the butler enters with a bouquet.)

Mendl: This is for Isabella Semyonovna, and there's a card enclosed.

Beylke: For me? (Takes the flowers)

Shimele: (Pleased) Flowers? Who sent them?

Beylke: (Reads the card) Solomon Oskarovich Fein. Ha, ha, ha!

Shimele: What's so funny? (To the butler) You can go.

Beylke: What do you mean? Isn't it funny? Presents all of a sudden — flowers? Where was he three weeks ago at this time, remember? When we asked him to do us a favor and put in a good word to his father about the rent, he shrugged his shoulders (Imitates him) and said, "That's none of my business!" (Hands over the papers to her father) The contract mentions everything you talked about. (Points to the pile of letters on the table) That's today's mail? (Takes the letters) I'm taking it with me. I'll give them back to you after I've read them. (Bows slightly to the young men, who jump up with a snap.)

Shimele: A strange daughter I have! Another girl in her place, with such a fur coat, such riches...

Eti Meni: At least say "knock on wood."

Shimele: A dress, a new hat, anything you want to buy her — she's not interested! What can you do? (The two young men show admiration.) What more could you want? She's been offered matches — the nicest, the best — she doesn't want to hear, she doesn't want to see. Can you imagine — Mr. Osher Fein, you've probably heard of him, he wants to make a match for his son with her — he's dying to! And his son wants to even more! And I want to still more, because I'd love to be related by marriage to someone like Fein. After all, I used to be his tenant.

SECOND ACT

Eti Meni: At least say "knock on wood."

Shimele: So what more could you ask for? Right? Since he wants it, and his son wants it, and I want it too, we could break the plates and that's it. Not with her, no! She says she needs time to think it over. (The two young men are impressed. Mendl the butler enters.)

Mendl: (Chewing on something) That no-good is here again.

Shimele: What no-good?

Mendl: Soloveitchik the matchmaker.

Shimele: Soloveitchik? Where is he?

Mendl: Over there. In the hall.

Shimele: Why doesn't he come in?

Mendl: I've already told you that this is not my first job in a rich man's house, and with rich people the custom is ...

Shimele: To announce the guests first. Well, you just did. Now go get him. (Mendl exits) God, this fancy etiquette the 'ristocrats have! If you want to know the truth, it gives me a pain in the neck, may God not punish me for saying so. (The door opens up wide. Mendl the butler lets Soloveitchik the matchmaker in. Shuts the door behind him.) Welcome, my dear matchmaker. Speak of the Devil! Sit down, Mr. Soloveitchik.

Soloveitchik: Is it ever hot today! Just awful! (Looks at the young men) And who are these young men? They look sort of familiar. (Comes back to him) Oh, yes! They're the ones from the theater, right? You're working on some deal with them — the whole town is talking about it. (Gives them his hand) How do you do? They say that you're scooping in money with both hands. (Gestures with both hands)

Vigdorchuk: Eh? Scooping in money is a little overstated. Thank God we earn enough to make a living.

Rubinchik: And manage to put away a few pennies too.

Soloveitchik: (To the tailor) Yes, I can tell you all about it. It's a lucrative business. It's like a well that never runs dry. People get rich! And they say they put away a few pennies. (Both young men smile broadly.)

Shimele: (To the matchmaker) You say that everyone in town knows about my film deal? Would you like to try some of our brandy? (Fills his glass)

Soloveitchik: What a question! The whole town knows about it and is talking about it, and everyone is jealous of you. (Drinks and takes some preserves)

Shimele: Jealous?

Soloveitchik: I should live so long and you and your wife should live so long too! Of course! Would I make up such a thing? People even say that you're about to become a millionaire... from their mouth to God's ear! (To the young men) Semyon Makarovich is a man who likes to do well and doesn't mind if others do well, too. As they say: Live and let live. (To the tailor) There's no help for it, Semyon Makarovich, things will go on and on for you. As the Bible says: when it rains it pours!

Shimele: (To his wife) Do you hear what he is saying? (Pours him another cup)

Eti Meni: (Looks at the bottle) I hear him — I'm not deaf. (To the matchmaker) What about the other business between you and us?

Soloveitchik: (To Eti Meni) What about it? Everything is fine — everything should go so well for all the children of Israel! (To Shimele and Eti Meni) When Soloveitchik gets an idea in his head, the whole world can turn upside down and

SECOND ACT

Soloveitchik will still have his way. I've just come from there, from the 'ristocrats. I got *some* reception: "How do you do"... "Take a seat"... "Would you care for a cigarette?"... "A cold drink perhaps — the heat must have made your mouth dry." It was really something! (Drinks up the second glass. Shimele brings him a pack of cigarettes.)

Shimele: Now then, so you've just come from the Feins. So how is it going?

Soloveitchik: It's going terrifically! I wish I could say the same about all my matches. Ah! when Soloveitchik, gets an idea into his head! (Takes a drag from the cigarette) If you're not too warm, I can tell you all about today's visit to the Feins: my arrival, the things I said, the things they said, what I said in reply, what they said in reply — the whole conversation. (Rolls up his sleeves, ready to tell the whole story)

Shimele: (Impatiently) What do I need to hear the whole conversation for? You know I'm just a simple fellow, and I like things just so — cut and dried. Just give me the bottom line.

Soloveitchik: The bottom line is — they're going to invite you to visit them. The whole 'ristocracy will be there. But first they will pay you a visit — possibly even today. That's Soloveitchik for you!

Shimele: (To his wife) Do you hear that? (Quietly) We have to prepare all kinds of snacks. (To the matchmaker) Are you sure they're going to be here?

Soloveitchik: (Swallows the preserves) As sure as my name is Soloveitchik!

Shimele: And the son too?

Soloveitchik: (Drinks the last drop) Of course!

Shimele: He told you so himself, the old man, I mean?

Soloveitchik: He himself, the old man, that is, said to me: "We will come by to visit the Sarokers, maybe even today. After all, he was once our tenant."

Shimele: Really, in those words? (To his wife) See to it that everything is ready. (Eti Meni exits.)

Soloveitchik: In those very words — I should live so long and so should you and your wife! What do you think, Soloveitchik is some kind of child? The only thing is, I have to exchange a few words with you in private. (To the young men) Excuse me. (Takes Shimele aside) I'll make it short — two words. (They stand near the edge of the stage.)

Shimele: (To Soloveitchik) I know what you want to talk about. You want to ask how much I'm giving for a dowry.

Soloveitchik: (Talks quietly) You should live and be well! What a mind! And you think perhaps that they want to know? Or that the groom wants to find out? God forbid! It's just that since it's nearer than farther — any minute, you know — if someone should ask me, you understand, I don't want to have to stand there like a dummy.

Shimele: You know very well that she is my only child, and after a hundred and twenty years, when I'm gone, it's going to be all hers.

Soloveytchik: I understand that, but about how much?

Shimele: There's fifty thousand rubles in cash in the commercial bank. Of course, there's a total of 150,000, but fifty thousand I've put aside for my daughter, and since she's my one and only child, when the time comes to go ... (The two young men eavesdrop.)

Soloveitchik: (Interrupts him) Nonsense! What is this talk? You'll live a long time yet, God willing! You have

SECOND ACT

to keep living, because you do a world of good. I know — good news travels fast. So there's fifty thousand in cash?

Shimele: No more, no less. I don't make empty promises. When I say I'm giving, I give. You follow me?

Soloveitchik: I've got it! We've got it all straight now, so I can go on my way. I have to run around and talk and talk. Goodbye for now and lots of luck. I'll see you, God willing, at the engagement. (To the two partners) I wish you half a million each and a whole million to your partner! So long — goodbye! (Exits)

Shimele: (To the young men) I hope you don't mind — in my house, people keep coming and going. Now let's get back to our business. (Puts on his glasses, rolls up his sleeves, goes to the table) Now I have to do the sensitive part — give away what we all like to keep. (Signs the paper. The two partners sign after him.) And now it's time to give the candies — the pile of coins. (Goes to the safe) But I must tell you, my dear partners, and don't tell anyone else, that I don't have much cash with me. True, I have a safe, but I don't keep such sums of money in the house. For that, you see, there's a bank. (Opens up the safe and takes out a check book) The commercial bank, that's where I keep all my capital. Whenever I need it, however much I need, I write a check and they give it to me. (Puts the check-book on the table) The only problem is, when it comes to writing Russian, I'm a little weak. For those things I have a daughter. She is, as you know, my head bookkeeper. (Eti Meni enters.) Call Beylke for a second. She has to do some writing for me.

Eti Meni: Isabellitchke? I think she went out. Let me go look. (Exits)

Shimele:	It's not good when you walk around like a blind man. When you can't write Russian, it's worse than walking around without glasses. (Pause) I'll tell you what — maybe you could be so kind as to write the check out yourselves. Who can write better? (Vigdorchuk and Rubinchik go over to the desk. Vigdorchuk picks up a pen and dips it in the ink. Shimele puts on his glasses, points to the place in his check-book.) Here on the right side, be so kind as to write in numbers, fifteen thousand: a one and a five and three — that's right, three — zeroes... And there below write, in letters, fifteen thousand. You don't have to add the word rubles, it's already printed there. That's right. Finished? And now be so kind as to pass me the pen, and once again I'll part with something precious. (Rolls up his sleeves. Sighs slowly, sweating) Ouf! I'm exhausted from this signing business today! And whose fault is it? My own father, may he rest in peace, is to blame. He didn't want to teach me how to read and write. If he had only let me learn how to write, I would be the greatest writer in the world. You can tell — I can grasp the essence of the most complicated business in the world with one glance.
Vigdorchuk:	(Takes his leave) You do have extraordinary abilities!
Rubinchik:	(Leaving) What a talent. Exceptional talent.
Shimele:	(Very pleased, shakes their hands) Really? It's a pity my wife isn't here, so she could hear what people say about me. (Gives the check to Vigdorchuk. Rubinchik reads the check. Vigdorchuk pokes his friend in the ribs with his elbow, puts the check in his purse, seems very nervous, buttons his coat, and gets ready to leave.)
Vigdorchuk:	I'm sorry we took so much of your time.

SECOND ACT

Rubinchik: We must have given you a headache.

Shimele: Don't apologize. After all, we concluded a business deal, with God's help.

Vigdorchuk: And a good one at that.

Rubinchik: A brilliant deal!

Shimele: So why are you apologizing? Let's drink to it. (Fills three glasses) Let's have a toast to the half million, and may it not be long before the whole town knows what a great deal we made. (They clink their glasses together.) Now you can go. Best of luck to you. (Shimele accompanies Vigdorchuk and Rubinchik to the door. Half a minute later Eti Meni comes in.)

Eti Meni: Beylke will be here in a minute. (Looks around) Where are those two no-goods? They already left? And who did the writing for you, or did you postpone it?

Shimele: What kind of postponement? I hate to put things off. With me, said is done, stitched and ironed, cut and pressed!

Eti Meni: Who did the writing for you?

Shimele: They did. I told them what to write, and they did it.

Eti Meni: (Claps her hands in dismay) They wrote it? Who knows what they wrote! Couldn't you wait for Isabellitchke? (At that moment Beylke comes in.)

Beylke: I beg you, please don't call me Isabellitchke. Call me by my real name, Beylke. That's my name.

Eti Meni: Listen to her! Now we've heard from the peanut gallery! Tell me, aren't we different from what we were?

Beylke: That's precisely the problem, Momma — that we're not the same as we were. Actually we are the same, but we think we're different. That's why we don't do what we should do, go where we should go, or receive people we should receive. Those who are our equals and our true friends, we don't let into the house.

Eti Meni: (To her husband) She's talking in riddles, so strangely — it's beyond me.

Shimele: (To his wife) How could you understand what we're talking about? (To his daughter) Nevertheless, one thing has nothing to do with the other. If the Feins invite us to visit, let alone if they come here to see us, I assume you will not refuse to see them. After all, the Feins are still the Feins.

Beylke: We'll see. I'll think about it. Either I'll go with you or I won't.

Shimele: (Upset) What do you mean you won't go? And who am I? Am I your father or not?

Eti Meni: (Tries to make peace) What's the fuss all about? The bear is still running in the woods, and they are fighting over the fur. The Feins haven't come to see us yet, they haven't invited us yet, and the engagement is still a long way off.

Shimele: (Even angrier) Great! Another one heard from! (To his wife) Who asked you to be the peacemaker? (To his daughter) We've never had a fight, and we're not going to start fighting now. We all know you can catch more flies with honey than with vinegar. Tell me, daughter, why is it that since God gave me the jackpot, you're dissatisfied, upset, and unhappy, as if I had never won the prize at all?

Beylke: What do you want me to do? Dance in the streets?

Shimele: Who said you should dance in the streets? I mean

SECOND ACT

	you ought to be more... (gestures with his hands) more alive... more, more... you know... more with it!
Beylke:	I'll tell you the whole truth, Papa. Since you make me say it, I'll say it. The whole thing leaves me cold. I don't enjoy it. Everything is a pain. Those I want to see, I can't — those I can see, I don't want to. I can't open my heart to you because you won't understand. You don't want to understand me, and you can't understand me, because the big prize has turned your head so far that you can't see the world around you. You take white for black and black for white.
Shimele:	According to you then it's really a misfortune that I won the jackpot?
Beylke:	One man's happiness is another man's misfortune. Your happiness is my misfortune. (Almost in tears)
Shimele:	(Repeats after her) Our happiness is her misfortune. (To his wife) What do you say to that? Can you make head or tail out of it?
Eti Meni:	(To her husband) You keep saying that I understand nothing, and you understand everything. She's trying to tell you, without saying it in so many words, that she doesn't want to go with us to visit the millionaires — she can't stand them.
Shimele:	Is that what you're saying? Well I say different! (Higher pitch) When I say go — we go! (Bangs on the table) And that's all there is to it, by God!
Beylke:	(Burying her face in her hands) I'm so unhappy! (Runs out)
Eti Meni:	Why did you have to say that? You've got her all upset.

Shimele: (As if burned by fire) Peti Meti! Don't get me angry!

Eti Meni: Are you trying to scare me?

Shimele: Shut up! Be more respectful! Don't you know who I am?

Eti Meni: Look who's putting on airs. You've lost your marbles.

Shimele: (Out of control) How dare you talk to me like that! Everyone takes his hat off to me when I walk down the street.

Eti Meni: They can take their hats off, not me. You may think you're a big shot, but to me you're just an ignorant tailor.

Shimele: Shut up or I'll show you who I am!

Eti Meni: The Hell you say! You should live so long!

Shimele: Tfu! (Spits)

Eti Meni: Tfu! (Spits) (Mendl the butler shows up at the door.)

Mendl: (Chewing) The guests are waiting in the other room.

Shimele: (Takes hold of himself) Guests?

Eti Meni: What guests?

Mendl: Mr. Fein and Madame Fein.

Shimele: (Suddenly sober) Why didn't you tell me? (To his wife) Ernestina Yefimevna! Tell them to put up some tea! Tell them to serve brandy and wine and preserves — all kinds of preserves! (Starts to go out to welcome the guests)

Eti Meni: (Holds him back) Where are you going? You want to receive your guests in a dressing-gown? (To the butler) Why are you standing there like an idiot? Can't you see he's wearing a dressing gown? Go bring him his coat! (Mendl exits.) I'll go welcome the guests in the meantime. (Fixes herself in front of the mirror and exits. Mendl the butler brings in a black coat and puts it on Shimele. Shimele buttons himself up, practices bowing, and rehearses his appearance before the important guests. Mendl stands behind him, imitating him. Shimele takes large steps to the door. Mendl follows him with similar steps.)

THIRD ACT
Scene 1

A foyer with a second curtain, so as soon as the first scene ends the second curtain can go up and the second scene can start, without an intermission. The foyer should be rather long, with a table and mirror, a coat-rack, and a stand for walking sticks and umbrellas. A clock on the wall and a few straw chairs. A closed door is painted on the curtain. One or two entrances from the sides. Mendl the butler stands at the painted door. Standing next to him, pleading, are the two tailor's apprentices, Motl Kasoy and Kopl Falbon, wiping their sweaty brows and trying to talk Mendl into letting them in. Mendl keeps his hands in his pockets, chews, and tries to look important.

Mendl: I want you to know that if it were anyone else, I wouldn't let myself be talked into it unless you first filled my hands with golden coins. Only then would I show you in, because... because you have no idea what a tough boss he is. (The two apprentices are surprised.)

Motl: Shimele Saroker, a tough boss? You must be kidding.

Kopl: You're pulling our leg.

Mendl: Pulling your leg? Not on your life! He's told me over and over that ordinary people in simple clothing should be kept out... and a craftsman, a tailor for example, should be dragged by the neck and kicked out bodily. (The two apprentices are amazed.)

Motl: Would you believe it?

Kopl: People change. Once a man gets into the money, he becomes a bourgeois like all other bourgeois.

Motl: (Takes out his purse, pulls out a coin, gives it to the butler) Here, have it your way.

Kopl: Just go and bring her out here.

Mendl: (Examines the coin, puts it in his pocket) So who do you want me to bring out here? Just her, the young lady, you mean?

Motl: Just her, just her.

Kopl: She's the only one we want to see.

Mendl: And what shall I tell her?

Motl: Tell her that two young men are waiting for her, that's all.

Kopl: Not just any young men, but the two men who worked with her for three years at the same table.

Mendl: (Chewing, thinks it over) No. That's still not enough. There are so many young men! I need names — names.

Motl: In that case, tell her Motl Kasoy and Kopl Falbon have to see her.

Kopl: That's it. Nothing more.

Mendl: (Repeats) Motl Falbon and Kopl Kasoy, Motl Falbon and Kopl Kasoy.

Motl: Not Motl Falbon and Kopl Kasoy, but the other way around.

Kopl: Motl Kasoy and Kopl Falbon.

Mendl: I see. And should I absolutely say "young men?" (The two apprentices start getting nervous.)

Motl: Meanwhile we're wasting time.

Kopl: And your boss could show up any minute.

Mendl: Don't worry about him — he's not home. He went for a walk to take care of some business, big business. He's bought all the theaters in town. All the theaters are ours from now on. If you want to go to the theater, you'll have to come to us first. (The two young men look at each other.) And

THIRD ACT

we'll let you in if we feel like it, and if not you'll just stand outside. No one fools around with us! (Realizes that the two young men are not impressed, so he tries harder) Do you know that we are richer than the Feins? They open their doors for us. First they sent the matchmaker to us three times a day — then they came in person — all for the sake of the match — they're dying to have it — they're dying to get our young lady — and their son is crazy about her — and she's head over heels in love with him, too.

Motl: In love?

Kopl: How long has this been going on? Since when?

Mendl: Since when? I don't know. All I know is that day or night, it's always "honey" and "dear," either he to her or she to him — kisses and hugs, hugs and kisses. What else can I say? Two young men — Kotl Fasoy and Mopl Falbon? Tfu! You've got me all mixed up!

Motl: Don't mention any names. Just say two young men and that's all.

Kopl: That's all.

Mendl: That's fine with me. I'm going. But what happens if the plague shows up?

Motl: What plague?

Kopl: He probably means Eti Meni.

Mendl: Eti who? Forget about Eti Meni! Anyway, her name is not Eti Meni any more, but Ernestina Yefimevna. (About to leave, then returns) Take a seat for a while, here, right here. (Shows them to their seats and leaves, chewing tobacco and repeating to himself) Mokl Fasoy, Fotl Falbon. (The two young men sit down carefully on the straw chairs and talk quietly.)

Motl:	A strange butler.
Kopl:	Very strange.
Motl:	Who should talk first, me or you?
Kopl:	You start. I'll join in.
Motl:	As soon as she shows up, you start talking.
Kopl:	Not me! Where would you start from?
Motl:	I'd start like this. (Stands up, coughs, rehearses with a trembling voice) "The reason we came, Beylke, the thing that brought us here has nothing to do with anybody."
Kopl:	"Only with you."
Motl:	Do you want to talk? So talk! (sits down)
Kopl:	No, you talk. Go on, talk!
Motl:	So why do you keep interrupting me? (Stands up, coughs extensively, puts his hand on his heart, goes on rehearsing) "This concerns only you, Beylke — your happiness, your fate, your whole life. We realize it's none of our business to interfere with your private affairs, but we couldn't sit still any longer since we learned that you, or rather they, are going to tie you up for life with a person who is not worthy of you — not worthy of living under the same roof with you, breathing the same air as you..."
Kopl:	Well said! And what if she asks you, what do we mean by that?
Motl:	I'll tell her the whole truth, that we've both been in love with her for a long time, and that we're dying to...
Kopl:	With all our heart! (Stops and cups his ear) Sh, I think she's coming.
Motl:	(Listens carefully) Who? Beylke? (Buttons himself

THIRD ACT

(up, gets ready to deliver his speech, coughs. Beylke comes in. The young men go over to her.)

Beylke: (Stretches her hands out to them) I'm so glad you came! God himself must have sent you! Where have you been for so long? I've been looking and looking for you. I almost gave up hope.

Motl: If you only knew, Beylke darling, how much trouble we've been having.

Kopl: They don't let us get near you.

Beylke: Who?

Motl: That guardian angel of yours.

Beylke: Ah! You don't know what this house has turned into. And there's no end to my troubles.

Motl: We've been trying to get to you. God knows how hard we've been trying to get to you.

Kopl: It's like trying to break through an iron gate.

Motl: (To Kopl) Don't interrupt me! (Kopl shuts up.) We wanted to tell you — you don't know how dear you are to us, how close.

Kopl: Like a sister, like our own sister.

Beylke: No, not now. This isn't the time for that. Now is the time to rescue me — you must help me escape.

Motl: We'll do anything for you...

Kopl: Through fire and ice!

Beylke: Wonderful! You have to rescue me; you have to help me get out of this house. You don't know what's become of this house. You don't know what's become of my father. Since he won the jackpot, he is unrecognizable. I had never seen him get angry before — now he gets terribly upset over the slightest thing — you can't say a word —

	you can't let out a peep! And the worst thing is that he wants to tie me up with that ... that ...
Motl:	We know — we've already heard — we know all about it.
Kopl:	That bourgeois? He shouldn't live to see the day!
Beylke:	He was just here. They were all here. They invited us over — promised that we would be ... but I said I couldn't come. Papa made a scene, complete with screaming and crying and anything you can imagine. But I stood fast, once and for all — no and no and no! What am I? A toy that you can buy and sell?
Motl and Kopl:	(Both at once) Right! Absolutely right!
Beylke:	I won't go! I won't go anywhere! I'll run away from them! I'll run wherever my feet lead me! I'd rather starve than ... (Puts her face in her hands, cries quietly)
Motl:	Beylke! Darling! Dearest! Don't cry! We'll help you.
Kopl:	Through fire and ice!
Beylke:	(Encouraged) You will? I knew that you'd come to my rescue. I'll teach them a lesson! I'll teach my parents a lesson! I want to give them the fright of their lives! I'll cause a scandal! I'll run away — in the middle of the night — not far, to the nearest town, the first train stop, but I'll run away just the same. Oh, will I scare them! Oh, will they look for me! Then I'll have it my own way with them.
Motl:	Beylke, what a smart girl you are!
Kopl:	The smartest!
Beylke:	Will you help me escape?
Kopl and Motl:	When?

THIRD ACT

Beylke: This very night! They're going to go to the Feins and I'll stay here. You be ready, right here under my window. (Motions with her hand) You'll have to get a buggy and you'll need some money. (Reaches for her pocket)

Motl and Kopl: (Together) Money? Who needs money? We have money.

Beylke: Remember, now — as soon as they leave I'll open the window. Shhh, my mother is coming! (Runs to one side. Eti Meni comes in from the other side. The two young men stand as if paralyzed.)

Eti Meni: (Looks them over) Look who's here! Kopl? Motl? I suppose you're here to see my husband? How are you doing? Who is your new boss? Sit down, why don't you sit down? As long as you're here, you might as well have a seat. So you want to see my husband? You can't see him today — or tomorrow either — the day after tomorrow is also impossible — because he's always so busy now. He has signed a contract for a whole company... a business... a big business... a very big business!

Motl: Yes, we know.

Kopl: We've already heard.

Eti Meni: What have you heard?

Motl: We've heard that Reb Shimon cut a big deal...

Kopl: Bought the whole town...

Motl: With all the theaters...

Kopl: And the hotels.

Eti Meni: (Surprised) Who told you about it?

Motl: Everyone...

Kopl: The whole town.

Eti Meni: The whole town?

Motl:	From one end to the other...
Kopl:	It's boiling, like a stewpot.
Eti Meni:	Their stomachs and hearts should only boil! How come they know so fast? I bet the matchmaker spread the news. What a big-mouth! Anyway, my husband — you can't see him now, but if there is something you have to tell him, you can tell me.
Motl:	It's not important...
Kopl:	We came just like that.
Eti Meni:	For a visit, you mean? Why not? Very nice of you. I can't stand beggars, God forgive me. No matter how much you give them or do for them, it's too little. They're like bottomless pits. So you have everything you need? That's nice to hear. And it's very nice that you remember your old employers. Drop by sometime. You know when? On the holiday, God willing. (The two young men stand up and look at each other.) My husband will have more time then. But don't talk to him about old times — it makes him uncomfortable. You understand — I don't have to spell it out for you. (The young men back toward the door, wiping the sweat from their brows.) Go and be well. Remember now — on the holiday, God willing, you'll come and be my honored guests. I'll serve you brandy and preserves. Goodbye now. (Eti Meni goes to the right. The two young men go to the left. Just at the door, they bump into Shimele Saroker who is coming in from the street with his coat and walking-stick.)
Shimele:	Welcome, guests! What are you doing here in the middle of the week as if it were the Sabbath? And how come you never show your face? Why in Heaven's name are you hiding?
Motl:	It's easier to get to the Czar than to you. We've

THIRD ACT

	been here a few times, but he never lets us in.
Shimele:	Who?
Motl:	That bone-breaker, your butler.
Shimele:	Don't listen to him. Just go right in. After all, you're my kind of people, cut and press!
Motl:	But he says you told him that if a tailor comes, he should throw him out bodily...
Kopl:	And let the Devil take him!
Shimele:	(Upset) I said that? When did I say that? (Takes the bell, shakes it forcefully as if the house were burning. Eti Meni comes running, frightened to death.)
Eti Meni:	Who is ringing like that? (Sees the young men) Are you still around? (They start to leave. Shimele stops them.)
Shimele:	I was the one ringing the bell. Where has he gotten to, our fine butler, that clown, that no-good?
Eti Meni:	What's the matter? What do you need him for?
Shimele:	I need him like a hole in the head. I just want to give him a good scolding, once and for all, so he'll stop kicking my guests out of the house. (To the young men) So how are you doing? I've missed you a lot — after all, we worked so long together in the shop. Come in, we'll sit and chat a bit and have a little drink, like old times!
Eti Meni:	The man has lost his mind! I won't let you have a single drop now. Have you forgotten that we have to get ready for an important visit? (Looks at her watch) It's time to get dressed. I'm sure Motl and Kopl won't mind. — they're like family — they won't mind coming back some other time.
Motl and Kopl:	(Relieved, in unison) That's right, some other time.

Shimele:	(Gives them his hand) My best wishes, and don't forget to come on the Sabbath. Come straight to me — don't ask anyone's permission — don't pay any attention to that demon at the door. If he doesn't let you in, show him what tailors can do, cut and press! (The two young men exit. Shimele exits on the other side. Eti Meni rings the bell. Yokheved the maid comes in.)
Eti Meni:	Listen, go get the broom, sweep up, and clean the place up.
Yokheved:	(Looks around) Where? It's pretty clean, I'd say. Where should I sweep? Where should I tidy up?
Eti Meni:	Maid, when I tell you to clean up, you clean up! You saw with your own eyes the two shlimazels who came by and left the dirt from their boots on the floor. Look at her asking questions! (Yokheved leaves with a shrug of her shoulder. Beylke comes in, a white bandage around her head.)
Beylke:	(Holding her head) What's all the ringing?
Eti Meni:	I was calling the maid. (Worried) Why are you holding your head?
Beylke:	It's nothing, Momma — it will pass.
Eti Meni:	(Even more worried) It's not a cold, I hope? You don't have a fever, do you?
Beylke:	No fever, just a little cold.
Eti Meni:	Do your bones ache? Or, God forbid, a pain in the side?
Beylke:	My bones don't ache, but I do feel a slight pain in the side.
Eti Meni:	(Wringing her hands) Woe is me — it's the flu! (Shimele comes in, wearing a white shirt on over his trousers and pulling at his collar.)

THIRD ACT

Shimele: (His head up. Doesn't see Beylke) Eti Meni — tfu! I mean Ernestina Yefimevna. Where are you? What kind of shirt did you lay out for me? With a collar to choke me to death. My eyes are bulging out. What am I supposed to do? Cry for help?

Eti Meni: Why don't you go take it off, and I'll give you another shirt. Why do you have to yell?

Shimele: (Clutching his neck) That's easy for you to say, another shirt. I can't put it on and I can't take it off. (Notices Beylke) What's this, a bandaged head?

Eti Meni: The child isn't feeling well. She has the flu.

Beylke: It's not the flu — I just don't feel well.

Shimele: (Forgets about the shirt) Why didn't you tell me? Go lie down! Call the doctor! (Rings the bell)

Beylke: What for? No need to call the doctor — it will pass. I'll go lie down — if I fall asleep, please don't wake me up.

Eti Meni: Go lie down, take a good nap. Nobody will wake you. (Beylke exits.)

Shimele: (Worried) Maybe we should call the doctor anyway? (Mendl shows up.) Go, Mendl, run and get the doctor.

Eti Meni: Later, when we come back from the visit. Now let her sleep for a while. (To Mendl) No need to call the doctor. (Mendl stays.)

Shimele: Suppose we postpone the visit.

Eti Meni: As far as I'm concerned, we need the whole visit like a hole in the head.

Shimele: What do you mean? And the match? I broke my back and banged my head against the wall, and now at the last minute the whole thing goes up in smoke?

Eti Meni:	In that case, go get dressed. (Yokheved comes in with a broom, a feather-duster, and a wet towel.) Look at that maid! You tell her to sweep the place up a little and she comes back with heavy artillery.
Shimele:	So what do you say? Shouldn't we call the doctor? (To the maid) Just a minute. (To his wife) Suppose it's really the flu?
Eti Meni:	You heard the child say she just wanted to sleep. She asked not to be awakened.
Shimele:	What a pain in the neck! What did I need the whole thing for? God! (Eti Meni and Shimele leave. Mendl the butler and Yokheved the maid silently look at one another and burst out laughing, louder and louder. The lights go out for a moment. The props on the stage are removed, and the second scene of the third act begins, without intermission.)

THIRD ACT
Scene 2

A rich household. The landlord, Mr. Osher Fein, a man with a well-established fortune, with a pot-belly and a bald head, taciturn, always with a cigar in his mouth, sits with three guests around a green table, playing cards. The other aristocratic guests sit around the players and look at the cards with great interest. The players say only a few words from time to time: "Seven spades." "Pass." "Six of diamonds." "Pass. Pass." At another table covered with all kinds of albums, big and small, sits Madame Fein. She is the exact opposite of her husband: pale and thin, but dripping with diamonds. She is surrounded by her guests, the wives of the aristocrats, all dolled up in expensive clothes and jewelry. The ladies sit motionless, like true aristocrats, and browse through the albums. Some sit closer to Madame Fein and talk to her in a low voice. The other ladies, who seem absorbed in the albums, follow the conversation with one ear and exchange knowing glances and grimaces.

Koltun has gotten very lavishly dressed for the occasion, with a tuxedo, a white bowtie, and white gloves. He has taken upon himself the role of supervisor, available for the guests, not as a servant, God forbid, but as a good friend of the family. He stands aloof, trying to look important. Soloveitchik the matchmaker is present too, dressed in his holiday finery, positively glowing. He can't sit still.

Madame Fein: You don't have to be beautiful, you don't have to be smart, you just have to be lucky.

First Lady: In relation to whom do you say that, Gertruda Grigorevna?

Madame Fein: (Ignoring the question) You see what I mean? My husband has had a pile of lottery tickets since I don't know when. So he never won. And that one, with all due respect, has no more than one ticket, but his one ticket had to win, and the jackpot at that! (The other ladies all exchange knowing smiles.) Can you believe it? I tell you, the day I heard that the grand prize had been won by that ... Saroker, I was thunderstruck. At first I couldn't believe it. Then when my husband and my Solomon came home and told me that they had seen Bank Director Goldenthaler with their own eyes and had heard from his mouth that the story was true, I felt, if I may say so, so bad I almost fainted. They had to put cold compresses on my forehead all night. I got some kind of spasm, so to speak ... And even now, when I think about it, I feel a chill run down my spine. (The ladies nod their heads in agreement.) Ay, yay, yay!

First Lady: They say his daughter is about to marry your son, Gertuda Grigorevna.

Madame Fein: (Letting this pass) It's the same with matches. I always prayed to God to send me a match from abroad, or from a big city, from a high-class family — A son like my Solomon — I don't have to praise him — everybody knows him. In the end, that devil, Love, poked his finger into the pie, with all due respect. (The ladies make faces, and one of them says quietly: A love of fifty thousand!)

Second Lady: Gertruda Grigorevna — is it true what they say — that he is giving a dowry of fifty thousand?

Madame Fein: And suppose he were to give a dowry of seventy-five thousand ... or even a whole hundred thousand? He can afford it — she's his only child. But you mustn't forget who he is, with all due respect, and who we are.

First Lady: But I hear that the girl is very beautiful ...

Second Lady: And talented, too.

THIRD ACT

Madame Fein: (Letting all this pass) If a matchmaker had come, and suggested this match, my husband would surely have thrown him out bodily. But now that Love, with all due respect, has interfered... (The door opens. Koltun comes in, looking both humble and self-important, and announces the arriving guests.)

Koltun: Semyon Makarovich Saroker! Ernestina Yefimovna Saroker! (Bows to them obsequiously with a broad smile. The tailor comes in wearing a new top-hat. His wife is bizarrely dressed in a multicolor dress. All eyes turn to them.)

Shimele: (Extends his hand to Koltun) How do you do, Yefim Panta... Panta...

Koltun: (Crosses his hands behind his back and answers quietly) Pantelemonovich.

Eti Meni: (Pulling her husband by the sleeve) Come on! Can't you find anybody better to talk to?

Shimele: (To his wife) It's just Koltun, our former rent collector. Don't you recognize him? (The landlord, Osher Fein, puts away the cards, stands up, and welcomes the dear guests. Madame Fein stands up, too. Solomon enters through a side door and comes over to the guests.)

Osher Fein: Welcome, guests! We've been expecting you for a long time. Why so late? Where is your daughter?

Shimele: (With his hat still on) It's her fault. (Points to his wife) When we were getting dressed, she couldn't find anything she liked. And when we were ready to go (Looks at his new suit) she says to me that she won't go if I don't put on a top-hat. So I say to her, what do I need a top-hat for? So she says: All 'ristocrats wear top-hats. So I say: If the 'ristocrats cut off their noses, will I have to cut off my nose too? (Takes off his hat. Koltun runs to take the hat from him. The tailor keeps his hat.)

A guest: Ha, ha! Cut off his nose! Very funny! (Everyone laughs. Soloveitchik steps forward.)

Soloveitchik: Ha, ha! Wonderful! When Semyon Makarovich says something, it's really something extraordinary.

Osher Fein: (Takes the tailor by the hand) Come, I'll introduce you to my guests. (Takes him to each guest separately and says loudly): Makar Semyonovich Saroker — I'd like you to meet Makar Semyonovich Saroker.

Shimele: (Interrupts him) I hope you don't mind my saying so, but you've got my name backwards. (At the same time, Madame Fein embraces Madame Saroker, kisses her cheeks, and introduces her to the other ladies.)

Madame Fein: So where's your daughter?

Eti Meni: She isn't feeling very well. I'm afraid she may have the flu.

Madame Fein: God forbid! What makes you think so? Sometimes people just don't feel well. I myself, with all due respect, was feeling sick for a week. (Seats the tailor's wife at the head of the table)

First Lady: (Softly) Aside from her indisposition, we should all have it so good!

Second Lady: All sick people should be so well!

Osher Fein: (To the tailor) Where is your daughter? Why isn't she here?

Shimele: She fell asleep — she has a cold. Maybe she inhaled some poisonous fumes. She stayed home, poor girl.

Osher Fein: (Seats the guests at the head of the table. Shimele

THIRD ACT

                makes himself very comfortable. The others sit down at the table. Mr. Fein brings Shimele a box of cigars.) What do you smoke? I mean, what do you prefer, cigarettes or cigars? Too bad your daughter didn't come!

Shimele: To tell you the truth, I don't smoke either cigars or cigarettes. But that's all right. As they say: You can't get too much of a good thing. (Takes a cigar)

A guest: Right! You can't get too much of a good thing. Ha, ha! Well said! (All the guests laugh.)

Shimele: (Bringing a cigar to his mouth) Who can give me a light? (Several guests reach into their pockets, and several matches are brought to him simultaneously.) Thank you very much. (Lights his cigar and puffs, but doesn't really smoke)

Soloveitchik: (Standing to one side, runs up to Shimele) Excuse me, you forgot to bite off the tip!

Shimele: Is this an essrog, and am I some pregnant woman, that I have to bite off the tip?

A guest: Some pregnant woman — ha, ha! (All the guests laugh.)

Soloveitchik: Wonderful! Ha, ha! (Meanwhile, the ladies are fawning over the tailor's wife. Someone brings her a chair, someone else puts a footstool under her feet, and someone else shows her an album. Madame Fein smiles broadly and sees to it that tea is served to everyone. Koltun serves the tea unobtrusively.)

Shimele: (Taking Koltun by the lapels) Yefim Pantalonovich, why are you running around like a chicken without a head? Stand still for a minute — I want to ask you something. Do you remember what you said just three weeks ago, that nobody has ever won with a lottery ticket since the world began? It's a fraud, you said! What do you say now? (Madame Fein is having a fit because her future in-law is engaging in conversation with her rent-collector. She signals to her husband to intervene.)

Osher Fein: Congratulations, Semyon Makarovich! They say that you've made a big business deal...

A guest: A deal in the millions.

Shimele: It's still a long way to millions, but, God willing, we'll get there too.

A guest: They say that you've created a syndicate of all the cinemas in town...

A guest: In America they call it a "trust".

Shimele: What they call it in America, I don't know. I just know that of all the businesses that I have been approached with, this is the best and the most respectable, and as for the millions — that's all in God's hands. (Blowing smoke) You can't imagine how many business proposals I've had. More than the hairs on your head. Literally everyone has suddenly become my best friend. It's remarkable! (The door bell rings. Koltun glides to the door.)

Koltun: (Announces) Henrik Feliksovich Himmelfarb!

Osher Fein: (Takes Himmelfarb by the hand, introduces him to the guests.) Henrik Feliksovich Himmelfarb, the bookkeeper of the Commercial Bank.

Shimele: An old acquaintance. (Gives him his hand) What's new?

Himmelfarb: Yes, an old acquaintance. (To Mr. Fein) I was the first to tell him the good news about the jackpot. (To the tailor) Wasn't I the first?

Shimele: The first, the second — let's say one of the first.

THIRD ACT

A guest: The first, the second — let's say one of the first. Ha, ha! Well said! (Everyone laughs.)

Soloveitchik: When Semyon Makarovich says something, it's really something extraordinary!

Shimele: (To the matchmaker) What did I say that was so remarkable?

Himmelfarb: (To the tailor) Anyway, you've never had any reason to complain about our bank.

Shimele: And the bank has no reason to complain about me. What I put in your bank, I wish on all the poor tailors in town.

Himmelfarb: (To the tailor) Most certainly. The question arises, therefore, what made you cast us aside all of a sudden? That's just plain ingratitude. It's like repaying good with evil. Mind you, you didn't ruin us, but it hurts our feelings. You see, we take pride in our bank. Ours is not some fly-by-night bank. Our bank could compete with the finest banks anywhere. For us to deliver 150,000 rubles is like — fu! (Makes a gesture with his hand)

Shimele: (Doesn't understand, drinks his tea, looks around) What's this scoundrel talking about? Can anyone tell me?

Himmelfarb: (Keeps talking) It's not that your money is so important to us. On the other hand, we were happy to have a client like you. Why not? But let me say that we did business before you came to us with the 200,000. The only thing is that we feel kind of hurt that you suddenly took out the whole sum, just like that.

Shimele: (Laughs heartily) What is he talking about? What kind of cock-and-bull story is this?

Himmelfarb: (Keeps on talking) When we first saw your check for that amount, we were a little upset. We wanted to send someone to ask you whether it was a mistake. But since we had heard that you were involved in a mammoth deal, a syndicate, a giant enterprise, we went to our Director, Mr. Goldenthaler, for advice. Our Director ordered us not to ask any questions and just deliver the money. But after we did, we could see that he was upset, and rightly so. Because however big the deal was, you didn't have to withdraw the entire 150,000 rubles in one day. So I assume you and your partners received some bonus from the other bank to which you are planning to transfer your account. I won't ask you which bank, because we're not afraid of competition. I'm just asking: What kind of bonus did you get? Tell me, please, in front of these people. (The guests begin to get curious. They encircle the tailor and the bookkeeper. The ladies listen from afar. Nobody understands what's going on, least of all the tailor.)

Shimele: (To Mr. Fein) How much does he say I took out of the bank, this little schnook?

Osher Fein: He says a hundred and fifty thousand.

Shimele: Ha, ha, ha! A regular clown! (To the bookkeeper) Young man, go home and get some sleep.

Himmelfarb: *You* get some sleep, old man — it's your time. I'm still a young fellow, and I've got a lot of living to do. I expect to have many a dance yet. You don't dance, Semyon Makarovich, but I do.

Shimele: So dance! Dance to your heart's content! But what's this hundred and fifty thousand you're talking about?

Himmelfarb: (Angry) Stop patronizing me!

Shimele: Stop what?

Himmelfarb: It's true that I'm younger, a lot younger, but I'm no little boy.

THIRD ACT

Osher Fein: (Trying to make peace) What's all the fuss? Simmer down!

Soloveitchik: I agree.

Himmelfarb: And secondly, why are you playing dumb? "What hundred and fifty thousand" indeed! Are you trying to tell me that the check that some guy named Kremenchuk or Romanchuk brought to the bank wasn't your check?

Shimele: It's not Kremenchuk and not Romanchuk. It's Vigdorchuk. He's one of my two partners, the ones I made the film deal with. I wrote him a check for fifteen thousand.

Himmelfarb: You can't bring yourself to say a hundred and fifty thousand?

Shimele: The problem is with you, not with me. I'm simply telling you what the check said.

Himmelfarb: If you want to tell me what the check said, then you have to say a hundred and fifty thousand rubles.

Shimele: What makes you say that?

Himmelfarb: Your check.

Shimele: Are you trying to tell me I'm crazy?

Himmelfarb: No, but you're trying to make me out a liar or a swindler, or you're just pulling my leg — God alone knows. (The guests get more interested and draw closer.)

Shimele: (A little worried) What do you say to this comedy? I write a check for fifteen thousand rubles, and this man comes along and tells me it's for a hundred and fifty thousand. This is a very strange business!

Osher Fein: From fifteen thousand to one hundred and fifty thousand is as big a difference as from cat to rat.

Soloveitchik: Hear, hear!

Shimele: What kind of fairy tales are you telling me? I wrote the check with my own hands. That is, I didn't write it myself, Vigdorchuk did, but I watched him closely when I signed it. (Writes in the air) One, five, and three zeroes.

Himmelfarb: (Writes in the air) One, five, and *four* zeroes.

Shimele: (Writes in the air) Three zeroes.

Himmelfarb: (Writes in the air) Four zeroes.

Shimele: Look at him, that Devil! Four zeroes, five zeroes, six hundred zeroes — doesn't it say explicitly, in words, fifteen thousand? So what do you have to say now, big shot?

Himmelfarb: (Loudly) What kind of fifteen thousand? What are you trying to tell me? It's says a hundred and fifty thousand rubles.

Osher Fein: Fe! I don't like the smell of it. (The ladies have all gathered together around Shimele. They sense that something important is happening. Eti Meni comes last.)

Eti Meni: What's going on here, Shimon, I mean Semyon Makarovich? (All the while this is happening, Koltun stands aloof, smiles with a malicious grin, and enjoys the scene. The doorbell rings. Koltun glides to the door and calls out.)

Koltun: Maxim Vassilevich Goldenthaler! (All eyes turn to the door for a moment. Osher Fein starts to introduce Mr. Goldenthaler, but Himmelfarb beats him to it.)

Himmelfarb: Wait — here's the Director in person. (To Goldenthaler) Maxim Vassilevich — how much was Mr. Saroker's check for, the one we paid out to that Mayerovich or Vigdorovich or Vigdorchuk — yes, Vigdorchuk?

THIRD ACT

Goldenthaler: (Coldly) A hundred and fifty thousand rubles. Why do you ask?

Shimele: (His eyes bulge) Eti Meni! What's happening? (Sees her, shouts at the top of his lungs) Gevald! Help! Run! Catch them! I've been robbed! They took everything! Help me catch the thieves! (Takes his hat and is about to run. The door opens, and Mendl the butler dashes in with a frightened expression on his face.)

Mendl: (Looks around) Has Isabella Semyonovna been here? No? Then you're in big trouble, boss! Your daughter left through the window and — pouf!

Eti Meni: (Wringing her hands) Woe is me! It's a catastrophe! I know what happened — I had a premonition it was going to happen. I should have realized when she said: Momma, I'll run away!

Shimele: (To his wife) Really? So why didn't you say anything? Dummy! Why didn't you tell me anything? (Holding his head in his hands) My daughter! My child! The hell with the money! The hell with everything but my child! (Takes his purse out of his pocket, tears off his golden watch with the chain, and shouts to his wife) Eti Meni! Take off your jewels! Give me your pearls! Your earrings! Your rings! (Eti Meni does as she is told. He puts everything in his hat and gives it to the guests.) People — here's everything I have. Do whatever you want with it. Just help me find my daughter. Help me get my child back. (Bursts out crying. Eti Meni cries with him. The guests look on, amazed.)

FOURTH ACT

An inn near a railroad station. Two rooms. One room, big and full of light, has two beds by the walls. The beds are made. A small table, a few chairs, a sofa, a mirror. Cheap pictures on the walls. A few vases with flowers in them. Two doors: one door leads to the street, the other, closed, leads to the other room. Motl Kasoy stands with his ear to the door. Kopl stands in the middle of the room. They speak quietly.

Kopl: (To Motl) Well?

Motl: (Moves away from the door on tip-toes) She's still asleep.

Kopl: Boy! I've never slept that long.

Motl: But think how frightened she was. She thought they were chasing us.

Kopl: How do you know?

Motl: She told me so.

Kopl: When?

Motl: Today. When you went to get some food and put up the tea, we talked for a little while.

Kopl: About what?

Motl: About everything...

Kopl: And about what's going to happen?

Motl: That too.

Kopl: So — what?

Motl: (Angry) What? You know what, so why do you ask? She's afraid that if her father catches up with us, we'll all get it, but good.

Kopl: So what can we do?

Motl: What can we do? We can marry her right

	away ... then, if he comes, he won't be able to do a thing. There's only one problem — who will be the lucky man?
Kopl:	(Scared) Of course! That's the whole problem.
Motl:	But we decided that long ago. Either we leave it to her, to Beylke that is, to say which one she chooses, or else we'll draw lots.
Kopl:	(Troubled) But meanwhile, hasn't she said anything? I mean, which of us ...
Motl:	Stupid! If she had told me, wouldn't I tell you?
Kopl:	That means the whole thing is still up in the air?
Motl:	(Looks upward) Yes, up in the air. But in the meantime it wouldn't hurt to get ready for the wedding and prepare everything we need.
Kopl:	Like what?
Motl:	Like a minyan, ten Jews.
Kopl:	That's no problem — you give them half a ruble and they'll come running.
Motl:	(Eagerly) You're right! A brilliant plan!
Kopl:	And if there's no rabbi around, any Jew can officiate, as long as he's an honest one.
Motl:	I swear, you've got a head on your shoulders! What a brain!
Kopl:	And if they don't have a canopy, four sticks with a piece of cloth would do — no problem.
Motl:	I could kiss you, Kopl. Go get everything ready, the way you said. You go, and I'll stay here. After all, we can't leave her alone.
Kopl:	God forbid! (Hesitates) The only thing is: shouldn't we find out first who's the one, and then go?
Motl:	What for, silly? We're running out of time, and if

FOURTH ACT

	Reb Shimon shows up ... You go and see to all the arrangements. Then, when you return with everything, we'll decide with her one way or the other, who is to be the lucky one. I can assure you — if you're the one, I'll wish you all the best. Why should I hold a grudge? We both want the same thing — to make Beylke happy.
Kopl:	Same here. If you're the one, it's your good luck, because the most important thing is Beylke's happiness. Well, here I go. (Puts his coat on) And you take care of her! (Goes to the door, stands there a minute, turns around, and then leaves)
Motl:	(To himself) What a fool! He still has hopes. It seems to me a blind man could see who she's in love with. (Listens) I think she's waking up. (The door opens and Beylke appears on the doorsteps, glowing and smiling.)
Beylke:	(Fixes her mussed hair and looks around) Nobody here? Where's Kopl?
Motl:	He went to bring people, a canopy, and everything else.
Beylke:	Does it have to be today, Motl?
Motl:	When else? Postpone it till tomorrow? And what if your father shows up?
Beylke:	Don't talk about that, Motl! I don't even want to think about it. (Comes closer to him) I only want to take revenge, to show them that I'm a person in my own right, a free person. Then they can come say whatever they want to say. Oh Motl, Motl — a Jewish girl can only liberate herself from her parents when she gives up her freedom to someone else.
Motl:	What's this talk about freedom? Who wants to take your freedom away from you? Beylke, my darling, didn't we swear true and eternal love to

each other? Weren't we bound to each other long ago, way before your father had the good fortune, or misfortune, to win the grand prize? We just didn't say it in words until the time was ripe. Now it seems as if one of us wants to go back on the agreement.

Beylke: (With ardor) I'll never go back on it! I'm just sad that I, their beloved daughter, have to celebrate my happiest occasion, the best day of my life, on the run, as if I were committing some crime. Don't forget, Motl, that whatever happens, my father is still my father and my mother is still my mother.

Motl: If we want to take pity on your father and mother, there are two possibilities: either we wait for them to come, or we turn around and go back home.

Beylke: God forbid! Then I'll really be lost. You don't know my father. You think he's the same man he used to be? May God not punish me for my talk, but since he won the jackpot, he's become a wild man. No! I have to do something that he won't be able to undo.

Motl: You mean that's the only reason?

Beylke: (Looks at Motl with a smile) Oh, Motl — what a funny guy you are. You want to make me say again that I love you more than anything else? Does Kopl know? Have you told him?

Motl: No, Beylke, I can't. I haven't got the heart. The guy is blind. Maybe he has hopes that he, not I, will be the one.

Beylke: (Sad) I feel for him. The guy is in love with me.

Motl: And how!

Beylke: What should I do? Should I talk to him?

FOURTH ACT

Motl: If you can. I told him that you would decide today, at the last minute, who would be the lucky one. And if you don't, I said, we'll draw lots. The one who wins will...

Beylke: (Laughs loudly) Ha, ha, ha! Ha, ha, ha!

Motl: (Surprised) What are you laughing about?

Beylke: I just had an idea. (Takes a white kerchief, makes a knot, then another knot) I have here two knots. Since you are older, I will give you the chance to draw first, so you'll draw the knot. Ha ha ha! (Steps are heard. Beylke goes to the window. Kopl comes in, drenched in sweat, carrying a load of packages.)

Kopl: You're awake, Beylke? (To Beylke) I hope you slept well. I ran all over the place. (Puts the down the packages, wipes away his sweat)

Motl: I hope it wasn't in vain?

Kopl: Oh no! In a few minutes a bunch of people will come with everything we need, the way we made up. (Points at the bags) And here we have something to nibble: honey-cake, herring, and liquor.

Kopl: Bravo, Kopl! You deserve a medal. Now there's only one thing left — we need a minyan and someone to officiate at the ceremony — a canopy, too. We're well supplied with honey-cake and liquor and snacks, and we have a bride also. There's just one thing: which one of us will be the groom? That's for you to decide, Beylke — it's up to you.

Beylke: This is very hard on me, very unpleasant. You know I am grateful to both of you — you've both done so much for me.

Motl: And we're ready do more...

Kopl: Through fire and ice!

Beylke: (As if she were considering something) Wait! You know what just crossed my mind? Let's draw lots.

Motl: That's just what Kopl and I have been thinking for a long time...

Kopl: Even before the misfortune with the grand prize...

Beylke: You see, all great minds run in the same channels! (Takes the kerchief, appears to make a new knot, and hands the kerchief to the two of them) Who is older?

Kopl: (Who was about to pull, to Motl) You are older, if I'm not mistaken...

Motl: By a year and a week.

Beylke: (To Motl) In that case, you should pull first. (Shows him the two ends. Motl seems to hesitate then pulls one end with two fingers and pulls out a knot. Beylke then puts away the kerchief.)

Motl: (Drops his hands and looks at Kopl apologetically)

Kopl: (Pale, sighs, speaks to Motl) Your luck! May God give you... (Cannot talk, tears choke his throat)

Beylke: Come on, Kopl — I didn't expect this from you. I thought of you as a good friend.

Motl: (To Beylke) He's not saying anything he shouldn't. Quite the contrary.

Kopl: Yes, quite the contrary. I should have half the good things I wish you for you. It's fate — the luck of the draw...

Motl: He could have won just as easily.

Kopl: Right. If I had won... Anyway, I wish you all the best.

FOURTH ACT

Motl: Amen! Come here, let me kiss you. (They embrace and kiss.)

Kopl: If you want to know the truth, I had a feeling it would be Motl and not me. How could it be me? I've always been unlucky, just plain unlucky. I have no complaints. As God is my witness, Beylke, I've always loved you, and I still do. And as for being Motl's friend — I tell you again, I should have half the good things I wish for you two. I had hopes — you can't blame me, I'm only human — but I realize1 that there was the other possibility, and if, God forbid, I should lose, I'd go right away to America. See? (Takes out a passport from his pocket) I got myself a passport. (Motl and Beylke look at each other, touched.)

Beylke; Why so far, all the way to America? Stay here, and let's all be good friends.

Motl: Don't forget, Kopl, it's Beylke who's asking you.

Kopl: We'll see. Meanwhile I'm still here, and I have to celebrate your wedding. After all, I'm almost like one of the family — on the groom's side.

Beylke: No, on the bride's side.

Motl: On both sides.

Kopl: Yes, on both sides (Listens) People are coming, people are coming. (Ten Jewish men, all different in appearance, come in. Some have hats, some have caps, some have long coats, and some have short jackets. One of them, with thick ear-curls and a yarmulke under his hat and with a red kerchief tied as a belt around his coat, will officiate at the wedding. Another, a bottle and cups in his hands, will be the sexton. Four others are holding four sticks, above which is a green cloth — this will be the canopy. A few women have also come in and are standing to one side with pious expressions, ready to give the response to the marriage-blessing. There are also a few children who have come to look at the ceremony and perhaps get a bite to eat.)

Kopl: (Signals to the Jew who will play the role of the rabbi) Well?

The Jew: Well what? (Signals to one of the women to lead Beylke to the canopy)

The Woman: Who is the groom? (Points to Kopl) You?

Kopl: No, he's the groom.

Motl: I'm the groom.

Woman: (Hands him a yellow kerchief) Be so kind as to cover the bride's face with this kerchief. (Motl takes the kerchief, goes over to Beylke slowly, and covers her face. The woman takes Beylke by the hand. She signals to Kopl that he should take the groom by the hand to the canopy.)

The Jew: And the ring? (The groom doesn't understand.)

The Woman: You know, a ring, a finger-ring. For the wedding ceremony.

Kopl: (Reaching into his pocket) A ring? I have it, it's here. (Takes out a paper from his pocket, unwraps a ring from it, and gives it to Motl)

The Jew: (To Motl) Put the ring on the bride's finger and repeat each word after me: (Says the words, and Motl repeats them) Harey as m'kudeshes li b'tabas zu k'das moshe v'yisroel...Mazel tov!

All: Mazel tov! Congratulations! (Motl and Kopl embrace. Suddenly the door opens. Shimele Saroker, Eti Meni, and Soloveitchik the matchmaker burst in. Great confusion.)

Beylke: (Falls into Motl's arms) My mother and father!

FOURTH ACT

Shimele: (Looks around, but doesn't recognize his daughter under the yellow kerchief) Where is she? Where is my child? Why don't you say something, people? For God's sake!

Eti Meni: Don't you hear her voice?

Soloveitchik: (Pushing through) Allow me, ladies and gentlemen. Here she is! (Rips the kerchief off Beylke's face) What do you say to that? Wonderful! This is really something!

Shimele: (Recognizes Beylke, goes to her with open arms) My darling daughter! Thank goodness you're alive, and I can see you again. (Beylke falls into his arms. Both are crying.)

Eti Meni: (Wrings her hands, sits down on a chair) Woe is me! It's a catastrophe! What have I lived to see? How have we earned God's punishment, that our child should disgrace us? What is happening here? Who is she going to marry? It's the end — my life is over!

Soloveitchik: (Who has quietly spoken to the Jews and found out everything, to Eti Meni) Begging your pardon, Madame, but you don't know what you're talking about. Your daughter has already gotten married, just now — to this guy. (Points to Motl) Mazel tov! Congratulations!

Eti Meni: (About to faint) Oh, my God! A bullet has struck me! An arrow right into my heart!

Shimele: Quiet! What are you wailing about, you silly woman? Dummy! If your child had died or converted, would that be better? Look what she's complaining about: her daughter has married one of our own, a tailor, a really fine fellow, and she's complaining. (To his daughter) Who is your beloved? This one or the other one? I'm not clear about that yet.

Kopl: (Points to Motl) He is the lucky one. We drew lots.

Shimele: (Surprised) What? A lottery?

Kopl: Since we were both in love with her, we drew lots. He drew the knot, so he came out the winner.

Soloveitchik: Wonderful! Didn't I say that one of these two would marry your daughter? I should live so long, and so should you and your wife!

Shimele: Why did you have to run away? You could have told me, and everything would have been all right.

Motl: Who could talk to you?

Beylke: Since the misfortune when you won the jackpot...

Shimele: What jackpot? What are you talking about? There's no more jackpot — we've been bled dry, down to the last penny. There's not even a trace of it. We're back to what we were, ordinary people.

Beylke: Who did it? Where? When?

Eti Meni: Those two no-goods from the theater.

Beylke: Vigdorchuk and Rubinchik? How did it happen?

Shimele: How it happened doesn't matter. They scooped up everything with both hands and disappeared. No one even raised an alarm. And don't think I didn't have a dream about it the night before, a premonition. My bad dreams should fall on their heads!

Eti Meni: Amen! Blessed be His Blessed Name!

Shimele: Well, enough of that. May the Devil take them! As long as my child is here, I am satisfied, and I'll lift my hands to God and say: "This too is all for the best."

Eti Meni: Amen!

FOURTH ACT

The Women: Amen! Blessed Be His Blessed Name!

Shimele: What's the big deal? Am I out of thread? God punished me because I wanted to become a millionaire — I wanted to be someone important. My head started turning, I was drunk with power, intoxicated. Now I'm sober again, and I can see I was a fool and deserved to be punished. (To the crowd) Good people, you've probably heard about the poor tailor who won the grand prize, two hundred thousand rubles? I'm the one. Shimele Saroker is my name. The two hundred thousand has faded away like smoke in the wind, and Shimele is back where he started. Now I'm celebrating a happy occasion — my daughter has just gotten married. Where's the honey-cake and liquor? Let's drink Lekhayim to our people, cut and press!

Soloveitchik: (Takes upon himself the role of toastmaster, and seats the bride and groom at the head of the table, then the parents, Shimele and Eti Meni) Follow me please. You sit at the head of the table. (To the others) Guests! To the table! (To Kopl) Fill the cups for the groom's side! (To the ladies) Ladies! Help yourselves to the cake and liquor! (Serves the cake and eats some himself. Points to the children) And give the little rascals a piece of cake too — it's a mitzvah. And it tastes good, too. It's really wonderful. Lekhayim, bride and groom! Lekhayim, father! Lekhayim, mother! Lekhayim to the groom's family and the bride's family! Let's live and be healthy and dance at the weddings of family and strangers! (Drinks. They all drink and eat.)

Shimele: Quiet! Listen to me! Today is a double celebration. First, because I found my child, my only daughter, my precious darling — she should be healthy and outlive me!

Eti Meni:	Amen!
The Women:	(Piously) Amen! Blessed be His Blessed Name!
Shimele:	The other reason is that she chose one of our own, my kind of people, and didn't want to have anything to do with that devil of a shmistocrat, who was so happy about the fifty thousand I was planning to give as a dowry, and which the two scoundrels robbed from my pocket, together with another hundred thousand — they should burn in Hell together with the money!
Eti Meni:	Amen!
The Women:	Amen! Blessed be His Blessed Name!
Shimele:	In that case, let's drink another Lekhayim in honor of the bridal couple and their friends, and in honor of all of us. (They clink glasses and drink.) And a very special Lekhayim to the one who chose my daughter. (To Motl) Lekhayim, Motl! May God grant you more happiness and joyous days than I have had!
Eti Meni:	Amen!
The Women:	(Piously) Amen! Blessed be His Blessed Name! (Motl and Shimele kiss each other.)
Shimele:	(Now very happy) Listen — hear me out, people! Since God has arranged that we should meet on such a happy occasion, it's only right that we should really celebrate and dance a little, as God has commanded. We'll take each other's hands, you'll sing with me, and we'll dance a little — some real folk dances. (The people stand around Shimele, clap their hands, and sing a happy tune, and the man who conducted the wedding and another man step forward and start to dance.)
Soloveitchik:	(Stops the first man) Tell me, old man, who are you?

FOURTH ACT

The Man: (While dancing) I am the man who performed the wedding ceremony.

Soloveitchik: And who is that other man?

The First Man: Just a man.

Shimele: Right! He's a fine fellow! A really fine fellow! (rolls up his pants and starts dancing)

Soloveitchik: And what about me? (He rolls up his sleeves and goes out on the dance floor with Shimon. The two of them jump and dance past one another, more and more vigorously and spiritedly. Then the woman who helped lead the bride to the canopy joins them and dances a kazatzka, swirling the yellow kerchief over her head. Kopl Falbon is unable to control himself and also dances a kazatzka. Everyone sings and claps hands. Shimele's voice can be heard above everyone else's.)

Shimele: Dance, people! Harder! Livelier! My good people, cut and press! My people!

CURTAIN

TEXT SOURCES

Dos Groyse Gevins — A Folksshpil in Fir Akten (The Jackpot — A Folkplay in Four Acts). Manuscript in the Beth Shalom Aleichem Archives, Tel Aviv.

Dos Groyse Gevins (The Jackpot). Di Zukunft, New York, February, May, 1916.

Dos Groyse Gevins (The Jackpot). Ale Verk Fun Sholem Aleichem (complete works of Sholem Aleichem.) Vol. 4. New York, Folksfond, 1917.

Amkha (Your People). Shalom Aleichem-Ketavim (works of Sholem Aleichem) Adapted and translated by I.D. Berkowitz. Vol. 6 (comedies). Tel Aviv, Devir, 1929.

Dos Groyse Gevins (The Jackpot). Adapted by Yankev Rotboym. Warsaw, 1973. Kept in the archives of the Polish Jewish State Theater.

BIBLIOGRAPHY IN YIDDISH AND HEBREW

Berkovitz, I.D. Harishonim Kivney Adam (The Classic Writers as Private People.) Tel Aviv, Devir, 1959.

Bialik Al 'Amkha' (Bialik on Amkha.) Haaretz, Tel Aviv, December 30, 1932

Boshes, Hada. Amkha, B'teatron Ohel (The Jackpot in the Ohel Theater.) Haaretz, Tel Aviv, May 8, 1964.

Bukhvald, N. Teater (Theater.) New York, Farlag-Komitet Teater, 1943.

Dinesohn, Yankev. Zikhroynes un Bilder. Warsaw, Akhisefer.

Dobrushin, I. Binyomin Zuskin. Moscow, Der Emes, 1939.

Dos Sholem Aleichem Bukh (The Sholem Aleichem Book.) Ed. I.D. Berkovitz. New York, Sholem Aleichem Bukh-Komitet, 1926.

Finf un Tsvantsik Yor Folksbine (Twenty-Five Years of Folksbine). Ed. I. Fishman, B. Levin, B. Stabinovitz. New York, May 1940.

Fogelman, L. Sholem Aleichem's Dos Groyse Gevins in Der Folksbine (Sholem Aleichem's Jackpot in the Folksbine Theater.) Forward, New York, February 2,

Ginzberg, D. A Farbenraykher Spektakel Ober...(Tsu Der Banayung Fun Dos Groyse Gevins in Yidishn Melukhe Teater) [A Multicolor Spectacle But...(Reflections on the Revival of The Jackpot in the Jewish State Theater)]. Warsaw, Folksshtime, May 16, 1964.

Gorin, B. Di Geshikhte Fun Yidishn Teater (The History of the Yiddish Theater.) 2 Vols. New York, Literarisher Farlag, 1918-1923.

Khashin, A. Der Sheferisher Veg Funem Moskver Yidishn Melukhe Teater — Tzen Yor Artef (The Creative Path of the Moscow Yiddish State Theater — Ten Years of Artef.) New York, 1937.

Litvakov, M. Finf Yor Melukhisher Kamer Teater (Five Years of the State Chamber Theater.) Moscow, 1924.

Liubomirsky, Yeshua. Der Revolutsionerer Teater (The Revolutionary Theater.) Moscow, Shul Un Bukh, 1926.

Manger, Itsik. Midrash Itsik. The Hebrew University of Jerusalem, 1969.

Manger, Itsik. Megile Lider (Songs of the Megile.) Tel Aviv, Amikam, 1976.

Markish, Peretz. Mikhoels. Moscow, Der Emes, 1939.

Mendele Moykher Sforim. Der Priziv (The Draft.) Petersburg, Zederboym, 1885.

Nahor, Asher. Amkha M'et Shalom Aleichem B'teatron Ohel" (The Jackpot by Sholem Aleichem in the Ohel Theater). Yediot Akhronot, Tel Aviv, May 10, 1964.

Niger, Shmuel. Vegn Yidishe Shreiber: Kritishe Artikeln (About Yiddish Writers: Critical Essays). Warsaw-Vilna, Z.S. Shrebrek, 1913.

Oyf di Lebensvegn (On Life's Roads). Moscow, Sovetski Pisatel, 1976.

Oyslender, N. Yidisher Teater 1887-1917 (Yiddish Theater 1887-1917). Moscow, Der Emes, 1940.

Rumshinsky, Yosef. Klangn Fun Mayn Lebn (Sounds From My Life). New York, Farlag A.I Biderman, 1944. A.I. Biderman, 1944.

Sachs, Arieh. "Noakh K'mashiakh, Shkiat Halets (Noah as Messiah, The Downfall of the Fool). Tel Aviv, Sifriyat Hapoalim, 1955.

Sefer Chemerinsky (The Chemerinsky Book). Tel Aviv, Laam, 1947.

Sfard, David. Shtudies un Skitsn (Studies and Sketches). Warsaw, Farlag Yidish Bukh, 1955.

Shayn, Yosef. Arum Moskver Yidishn Theater (Around the Moscow Yiddish Theater). Paris, Les Editions Polyglottes, 1964.

Shmeruk, Khone. Shalom Aleichem: Ketavim Ivriim (Sholem Aleichem: Works in Hebrew). Jerusalem, Mosad Bialik, 1976.

Vonvild, I. Editor. Bay Undz Yidn (Among Us Jews). Warsaw, Di Velt, 1923.

Yablokoff, Herman. Arum der Velt Mit Yidish Teater (Around the World with Yiddish Theater). Vol. 2. New York, 1969.

Yidisher Teater in Eyrope Tsvishen Beyde Velt Milkhomes (Yiddish Theater in Europe Between the Two World Wars). 2 Vols. New York, Congress for Jewish Culture, 1968.

Zusman, E. Amkha (Your People — The Hebrew title for The Jackpot). Davar, Tel Aviv, December 23, 1932.

Zylbercweig, Zalmen. Lexicon Fun Yidishn Teater (Lexicon of the Yiddish Theater). Vol. 4. New York, Farlag Elisheva, 1963.

BIBLIOGRAPHY IN OTHER LANGUAGES

Artaud, Antonin. Le Theatre et Son Double (The Theater and Its Double). Saint Amand, 1970.

Barna, Yon. Eisenstein. Bloomington, Indiana University Press, 1973.

Bergson, Henry. Le Rire (Laughter). P.V.F. Vendome, 1975.

Catholy, E. Fastnachtspiel. Metzler, 1966.

Chagall, Marc. My Life. New York, Orion Press, 1960.

Duchartre, Pierre Louis. The Italian Comedy. New York, Dover Publication, 1966.

Frye, N. Anatomy of Criticism. Princeton University Press, 1975.

Gorchakov, A. Nikolai. The Theater in Soviet Russia. Freeport, Books for Libraries Press, 1972.

FOURTH ACT

Ionesco, E. Notes et Contre Notes (Notes and Counter Notes). Saint Amand, Gallimard, 1975.

Kowzan, Tadeusz. Literature et Spectacle (Literature and Theater). Warsaw, Mouton, 1975.

Max Reinhardt and His Theater. Ed. Sayler. New York: M. Oliver Brentand's, 1924.

Max Reinhardt und Sein Theater in Bildern (Max Reinhardt and His Theater in Pictures). Salzburg, Max Reinhardt-Forschungsstatte.

Meyerhold on Theater. Translated and edited by E. Braun. Chatham, Methuen, 1969.

Das Moskkauer Judische Akademische Theater (The Moscow Jewish Academic Theater). Berlin, Die Schmiede, 1928.

Mukarowsky, Yan. Structure, Sign and Function. Yale University Press, 1978.

Saussure de, Ferdinand. Cours de Linguistique Generale (Course in General Linguistics). Paris, Payot, 1975.

Seelmann-Eggebert, Ulrich. Zweites Gastspiel des Warschauer Judishen Theaters in Basel — Erinnerung von Vergangene Zeiten" (Second Performance of the Warsaw Jewish Theater in Basel — Memories of Bygone Times). Basler National Zeitung, March 5, 1976.

Ubersfeld, Anne. Lire le Theatre (Reading the Theater). Zwickau, Editions Sociales, 1978.

Veinstein, Andre. La Mise en Scene Theatrale et Sa Condition Artistique (Directing in the Theater and its Artistic Condition). Paris, Flammarion, 1955.

Waife-Goldberg, Marie. My Father, Sholem Aleichem. New York, Schocken Books, 1971.

Walter, Erbew. Marc Chagall. London, Thames and Hudson, 1966.